The Shifting Sands of the Internet: Adapting to Heterogeneity and Emerging Demands

Michael

Contents

Chapter 1

Introduction

The prevalent architecture of today's Internet has undergone a massive change in the requirements since its inception. The initial requirement was mainly to support resource sharing. This formed the basis for the current design of Open Systems Interconnection model (OSI) model and the TCP/IP protocol suite [4]. The communication in a TCP/IP network necessitates a binding association of *what* the user wants to *where* it is located. The resulting communication pattern involves a point-to-point connection between two entities identified with their respective IP addresses. Internet has attracted the interest of larger population and an estimated 4.1 Billion people across the world are using the Internet today [5] (5.3% increase compared to 2018). Thus, the current utilization of Internet and its services continue to evolve beyond its initial requirements to accommodate the needs of users.

However, users are increasingly becoming interested in receiving the content they desire irrespective of its location. This shift in the use of Internet has resulted in many research efforts towards designing architectures and applications that caters to the present needs. Accordingly, many new architectures like Information-Centric Networking (ICN), Internet of Things (IoT), Wireless Sensor Networks (WSN), 5G, Cloud and Edge computing have emerged. Further, newer applications and services like video streaming, data analysis, Artificial Intelligence (AI), smart cities, autonomous driving, data centers, SDN, SFC, NFV, *etc.*, are developed to operate in these heterogeneous networks. However, many of these applications are expected to operate across the heterogeneous networks to widen their scope and reach consumers across these networks. Nevertheless, these networks operate with different protocols and enabling seamless communication across them is an on-going research challenge. Moreover, there are many open problems within these heterogeneous networks that are yet to be resolved so they can evolve and thereby accommodate the requirements of existing and upcoming applications. Therefore, PHOENIX analyzes the heterogeneous and evolving Internet architectures with exemplary applications to discuss open problems and devise efficient solutions to resolve them.

1.1 Evolution of Internet architectures

Users seek information available in the network regardless of its location, provider or the mechanism of retrieval. The process of information retrieval can be considered to comprise two steps in an IP-based network: *1) name resolution*: which maps the identifier of the content such as the Uniform Resource Locator (URL) to its current location (IP address), and *2) location based forwarding*: which involves forwarding in the network to reach the object or to retrieve the data. The name resolution (usually a DNS lookup) is performed in the application layer prior to forwarding. This *early binding* potentially wastes network resources if there are alternate sources for the content. It may also result in poor user experience since consumers cannot get the content even if there is a nearby copy available. In addition, such an approach may not be able to take advantage of in-network caching as the network has no understanding of the request for a content that has multiple copies.

To address the above mentioned shortcomings, ICN treats content as a first-class entity. Many new networking architectures have been proposed under the framework of ICN, including Named Data Networking (NDN) [3,6], MobilityFirst (MF) [2] and eXpressive Internet Architecture (XIA) [7]. They share the same goal of name based, location independent communication but with different approaches. The quintessential part of these architectures is the use of *identifier of content* to seek the content of interest. With the ability of the network to understand the content, these solutions are able to integrate name resolution in the network layer either in-path (NDN) or off-path (MF). Since each router can understand and decide the direction to forward the requests (also known as *late binding*), the network is able to find better sources for the content. This reduces the latency and load on network and providers. ICN solutions also integrate in-network caches which further optimizes the efficiency of the network due to its content awareness. Further, security is enhanced in ICN since it embeds security in the content rather than on the communication link. Moreover, ICN also supports multicast and broadcast features without additional overhead. Hence, ICN is a more suitable candidate to address the current needs of users in the Internet.

In recent years, IoT has become a growing topic of interest and has drawn the attention of academia and Industry. IoT refers to a network of devices like machines, vehicles, electronic appliances, and also wearables like Radio Frequency IDentification tags (RFID), Step-counter, *etc.* These devices are usually embedded with sensors, actuators, memory and network connectivity. They are mainly used for sensing, monitoring and controlling various applications. It is important to understand the difference between IoT and *Sensor Networks*. There are various heterogenous *Sensor Networks* that operate in their own private network. The goal of IoT is to provide the *Sensor Networks* access to the Internet to realize IoT [8]. From their inherent design we can observe that in IoT, the devices are interested in the content and not their location *i.e.*, IoT is information centric in nature; hence, the design of ICN suits fairly well for IoT. Therefore, many ICN architectures like NDN [6], MF [2], *etc.*, are focusing on how IoT could benefit with ICN. Additionally, it is feasible for ICN architectures to be deployed in a closed domain like IoT compared to a full-fledged deployment in the Internet.

In addition, nowadays the mobile Internet access has become prevalent with 6.38 billion mobile broadband subscriptions in 2019 [9]. Recent advancements in technology have allowed the hand-held/portable devices to dominate the market. These devices introduce mobility that in turn raises challenges for the underlying network to support them. The recent advancements in IoT and trend towards 5G [10] are expected to increase the demand and challenges for supporting mobility. Further, Billions (50 Billion by 2020 [11]) of IoT devices are expected to be connected in the near future to realize many future applications including smart cities, smart industries, *etc.*, and many of these nodes could be mobile. Hence, mobile traffic will soon dominate majority of traffic in the Internet and is introducing new challenges for efficient data transmission in and across the networks.

Due to the availability of advanced networks, low-cost computer hardware and storage along with virtualization and new business models, Cloud computing (i.e., network of data centers) has emerged to provide flexible, low-cost storage and computing power to its end users. Cloud can be used to run complex analysis and provide services to fulfill the requirements of many businesses and applications. However, due to is inherent design and the rapidly increasing traffic that contends for the core network bandwidth, Cloud is unable to fulfill the requirements for low latency and low response delay [12] that are crucial for many applications like, video streaming. Thus, an increasing trend is to push the processing to the Edge/Fog [13] to efficiently utilize the network and fulfill applications requirements. Further, Edge/Fog computing improves the Quality of Service (QoS) experienced by users through deploying the required storage and computing at the edge of the network close to the users. Many applications, including but not limited to smart grids, sensor networks and industrial automation have been realized with Edge/Fog computing. Moreover, deployment of the future architectures like ICN can greatly benefit with Edge/Fog computing as it expedites the process of integration with the existing technologies and exploits the heterogeneity of the devices available at the edge.

In addition, with advancements in computing power and availability of Big data, the branch of AI has gained increasing momentum in recent years. AI is the interdisciplinary field which is redefining the landscape of existing architectures and generating opportunities for developing new applications and services. Hence, many new applications are emerging through employing the machine learning and deep learning algorithms [14–16]. Furthermore, deep learning has revolutionized the field of computer vision applications and is used in a wide range of applications including speech and image recognition, language processing, video analysis, text analysis *etc.* With recent advancements in the field of computer vision and deep neural networks, highly accurate models are now available to classify and detect objects in images and videos. Thus, research and business institutions have realized the potential for applying the AI principles to evolve existing networks and thereby support the creation of newer and more efficient applications and services.

1.2 Open research problems

This section discusses the high level open research problems and challenges that are addressed in PHOENIX.

1.2.1 Impact of naming schema on the performance of ICN

ICN treats content as the first-class entity and nodes exchange information based on the identity of the content irrespective of the location. There is an increased availability of data in ICN due to in-network caching and security is also enhanced since ICN embeds security in the content rather than on the communication link. The naming schema is the primary differentiator among the recently proposed ICN architectures like NDN which uses hierarchical names compared to MF and XIA which use (self-certifying) flat names for naming the content. Intuitively, hierarchical names provide the benefit of *aggregation* potentially leading to a smaller routing table size and reduced storage and computation requirements on the router (scalability). Hierarchical names also provide rich semantics. *E.g.*, a user can request the first packet of the latest version in a file by specifying `/fileName/_maxVer/_minSeg` where the `_maxVer` and `_minSeg` are indicators to routers on how to forward the data. In a publish/subscribe (pub/sub) system with hierarchical names, users can also indicate the granularity of the subscription. *E.g.*, a subscriber subscribing to `/sports` can receive content which is a descendant of this name, such as `/sports/football/...`, `/sports/ basketball/...`, *etc.* On the other hand, the lookup of flat names is more efficient compared to hierarchical names. A simple hashtable/bloomfilter lookup can determine the next hop for a content request. Backbone routers can also take advantage of parallel processing by partitioning the name (or hash) space based on the number of cores. Nonetheless, supporting the content identity space is not easy even in modern routers with memory of up to several gigabytes. The number of contents is estimated to be one to two orders of magnitude larger than the current IP address space [17] but the name space can be even larger. The choice of a naming schema is an intrinsic and fundamental aspect of each ICN solution, as it can affect the forwarding efficiency, scalability, manageability and other aspects of the overall architecture. There is a need to analyze the performance of hierarchical *vs.* flat names in an ICN environment to better understand the impact of naming schema in the network and address the resulting challenges.

1.2.2 IoT: seamless integration of heterogeneous *Sensor Networks* to the Internet

The IoT devices are deployed extensively in smart buildings, smart offices, smart homes, autonomous vehicles, industrial automation, environmental monitoring, *etc.* Billions of IoT devices are expected to be connected in the near future to communicate, sense and gather data. Currently, IoTs are designed to operate with the IP architecture [18]. However, IoT networks often contain many resource constrained devices with smaller memory, limited computational capacity and power supply (mostly a battery). Many IoT applications require devices to operate for longer periods in remote locations with no facilities *e.g.*, forests. Due to constraints, IoT devices are equipped with Layer 2 technologies like IEEE 802.15.4 and Bluetooth LE; hence, they operate with a much smaller Maximum Transmission Unit (MTU)(127 bytes) than the current MTU used in the Internet (1500 bytes). They also incur several other challenges like limited IP address space, while point-to-point connectivity is heavy for these resource constrained devices. Additionally security is another critical aspect in many IoT applications and it is expensive (induces overhead) to achieve with IP leading to complexity in operation and resource consumption. Therefore, there is a need for an efficient design for connecting the various heterogeneous *Sensor Networks* to the Internet to realize IoT. The design should provide a scalable, efficient and secure mechanism for communication across the heterogeneous networks to gather data for monitoring and/or controlling purposes [19].

1.2.3 Light-weight publish/subscribe system for IoT

Pub/sub systems have acquired a substantial portion of the Internet traffic with steady increase in popularity. In a pub/sub system, the *publishers* produce content and classify them into categories. Publishers merely produce the content and do not have any knowledge of the receivers called *subscribers* interested in the content. Similarly, the subscribers do not have any knowledge of the publishers or when the content of their interest will be published. Subscribers express their interest in receiving content from certain categories of their interest and receive the content as and when it is published. Interestingly, the communication in IoT environments also mostly follows the pub/sub paradigm where the sensor devices periodically sense and produce the data while an interested node like the Base Station (BS) collects this data. The sensor devices are only interested in producing the sensed data. These devices are not aware of whom this data is targeted for or how it is used. Similarly the BSs are not aware of the devices that are producing the data; they are merely interested in the data.

The pub/sub systems have been known to provide greater network scalability, large scale information dissemination and dynamic network topology. Although, ICN is suitable for IoT and the design of ICN proposals like NDN supports efficient query/response capability, authors in COPSS [3] point out its limitation to support pub/sub efficiently. They propose a content oriented publish/subscribe system called COPSS to enhance NDN with an efficient pub/sub capability. However, IoT does not need the full CCN/NDN+COPSS stack. Some other works like CCN-lite/NDN-lite [20] support more specifically the resource constrained IoT devices. However, like NDN, CCN-lite/NDN-lite lack support for pub/sub capability. There is a need for a light-weight, efficient and scalable pub/sub system for supporting the communication in IoT environments.

1.2.4 Network mobility in ICN

During mobility, a change in the physical location in IP leads to a change in the IP address with the additional pit-fall of breaking on-going sessions. Intensive research has been made and is on-going in the networking community to support mobility. As a result, in recent years, many overlay solutions involving complex and less-efficient techniques comprising dedicated resources, anchors and tunnels have been proposed. However, as discussed earlier, the recent advancements in IoT and trend towards 5G [10] are expected to increase the demand and challenges for supporting mobility in the network. Hence, mobile traffic will soon dominate the majority of traffic in the Internet. For ease of management, the networking infrastructure is usually organized into segments/domains. It is not un-common for a segment of the network to experience mobility. *E.g.*, a moving car equipped with numerous sensor/IoT nodes or a moving passenger train with WiFi connectivity for its passengers. The challenges associated with mobility are further compounded with such scenarios where the network/domain itself is in motion. In these scenarios, the end-nodes/users within these networks could behave both as the producer and consumer of the content. In principal, a moving train/car constitutes a network-on-the-move[1]. This **book** envisions that domain mobility will be a norm in the

---

[1] network-on-the-move refers to a mobile network in PHOENIX.

near future. With network-on-the-move, the network will incur increased signalling traffic and global updates could consume a large portion of the network traffic. Global updates, anchor-based and anchorless solutions generate ~0.215B mobility updates (see §8.4.2) during deterministic network mobility for a dataset with 1M names and 243340 mobility update during non-deterministic mobility update with just 200 cars. The resulting global updates might be too slow for latency sensitive applications resulting in increased loss of connectivity and packets. Overall, increase in network mobility could lead to poor performance and below par user experience.

Many recent works like [21–23] propose various solutions for addressing producer mobility in ICN. Nonetheless, support for network-on-the-move remains a largely untouched area of work. A network-on-the-move also differs from a mobile host that advertises multiple prefixes. The mobile host advertising multiple prefixes will produce the same content, but with many names. Hence, duplicate copies of the content will be stored in the caches but with different names, which is not exactly aligned with the ICN principles. Further, such solutions also affect aggregation in the network [24]. Although there are IP based network-on-the-move solutions such as Nemo [25] and MobileIP [26], they cannot be directly adopted in content centric ICN [27] environments. Therefore, there is a need to support network-on-the-move in ICN to address the challenges incurred due to mobility.

1.2.5 Resource-accuracy optimization with supervised deep learning models

Nowadays, data analysis such as video analysis, image analysis, text analysis, *etc.*, have become popular applications due to recent advancement in technology, AI and widespread availability of Big data. These applications demand high computing resources and storage. Hence, Cloud computing environments have become a common platform to host such analysis applications to provide the necessary services like storage, analysis and cost-effective scalability. Studies [28, 29] have shown that video analysis is fundamental, but a time consuming, resource demanding, expensive and latency sensitive component of the video analysis applications.Videos contain complex temporal information, and hence, they are significantly more difficult to collect, store and analyze than static images and text documents. However, many of the recent works [14,28,30–32] mainly focus on static image analysis for detecting objects in an image. Therefore, they cannot be directly applied for complex video analysis operations like video classification where a given video is classified into several classes based on its content. During video analysis the network must process several frames at a time while maintaining the temporal relationship with respect to each frame in the video. Thus, video analysis, especially, classification is non-trivial and demands more computational resources than object detection in static images or text-based analysis. Hence, deep Neural Networks (DNN) is increasingly used during video analysis to improve the accuracy of predictions. However, DNNs are computationally intensive and expensive. During analysis, there is always a trade-off between the *resource demand* and *prediction accuracy i.e.*, highly accurate DNNs also demand higher computing resources [14]. Therefore, profiling is used extensively to improve the performance of video analysis [28, 30, 31] and achieve better resource-accuracy trade off. Profiling refers to an operation of selecting the optimal configurations empirically for the DNNs to improve the inference/prediction accuracy during video analysis. Whereas, a configuration refers to a combination of knobs like, the frame rate, resolution, and detection model.

Many previous works [28, 30, 31] profile the configurations at the beginning of video analysis. While recent approaches [14, 32] use dynamic re-profiling during on-going video analysis to further improve the accuracy. However, profiling is an additional overhead incurred by video analysis applications besides the complexity of DNNs. The associated complexity of profiling grows exponentially with the increasing number of knobs in the configuration [14,32] and their corresponding values. For instance, analyzing a simple video with few knobs could result in thousands of possible configurations. Zhang *et al.* [32] also showed that, cost of profiling was 52x for a one second video and they used 5 GPU's with parallelization and sampling to speed up analysis. Nonetheless, optimizing profiling to improve the accuracy is not enough. There are many other aspects to video analysis and DNNs such as processing, resource, latency, bandwidth utilization and storage that needs to be examined for improving the performance and optimize the resource-accuracy trade off.

1.2.6 Real-time security with unsupervised deep learning models

To ensure the security of any online application, it is essential for organizations to detect and mitigate malicious activities on their networks such as, unauthorized access, malwares, port scanning, etc. These attacks may allow unauthorized access to the network and inflict further damages like compromising credentials, violating intellectual property rights, etc. Furthermore, such attacks may even expose business sensitive information including confidential documents of government agencies, resulting in serious security breaches [33]. The reported losses incurred due to security breach in 2011 by RSA and Target corporation in 2013 were \$66 and \$248 million [34, 35]. Therefore, system logs are commonly used to periodically record states of the systems and any significant events at various points. Nearly all computer systems today collect and maintain such system-wide log data. These logs are used by system experts to diagnose suspicious behaviours like system failures, unauthorized authentication, *etc.* Analyzing the system logs is essential to discover the root cause of any problem and potential security breaches. Hence system logs are a valuable source of information and they are crucial for monitoring online applications and detecting anomalies. However, even though operations like log data analysis and storage are essential, they tend to be expensive, especially in large scale networks. Due to the rapidly increasing number of Internet applications and users, the size of log data collected by a system running on even a medium-sized network can grow beyond terabytes per day. Until recently, about 500 MB of logs per day was considered a normal volume in small businesses; today, 5 GB per day is not unusual for such environments. Large organizations can easily produce logs that are orders of magnitude larger than this. Hence, such vast amount data generated everyday necessitates the need for an efficient strategy to store, analyze and manage the system logs.

Studies in [36] show that an application running on 51,000 Amazon EC2 instances and publishes five custom metrics will incur a charge of $31,646.40 per month [37]. Therefore, it is challenging and nearly impossible to do manual analysis in real-time and traditional approaches such as mining are proven to be in-effective. Besides, since log data mainly follows a time-series distribution, it is subject to rapid updates. Therefore, obtaining labelled log data for any applications area of interest is often difficult and it is mostly unbalanced or system specific; hence, it needs to be pre-processed before analysis. In addition, obtaining a large-scale log anomaly dataset with high-quality ground truth has been an on-going challenge [38–40]. Labelling log anomalies in a dataset requires expert's assistance and therefore it is labor intensive and often expensive. Hence, supervised machine learning strategies like [38–40] that depend on prior patterns of normal and abnormal behaviours are not suitable for real-time anomaly detection systems. Many recent works like [33,41], propose unsupervised machine learning algorithms for detecting anomalies. However, these unsupervised machine learning approaches train the models offline and hence, they cannot effectively adapt to the rapidly changing network behaviours over time and learn new threats and vulnerabilities. With the increasing arrival of newer and innovative threats, the models trained offline can soon become outdated and put the system at risk. Therefore, recently, Du et al. [36] proposed online log anomaly detection to generate sequences leveraging Long Short-Term Memory (LSTM) [42] or clustering algorithms for detecting Denial of Service attacks. Some others [43–45] leveraged LSTM networks to pre-process the sequence of API calls as components in order to detect malwares in the system. However, these approaches also suffer from increased latency and pre-processing overhead and thus are not suitable for detecting anomalies rapidly. Therefore, there is a need for efficient online log-anomaly detection system that addresses the above mentioned challenges and detects anomalies in real-time with high accuracy.

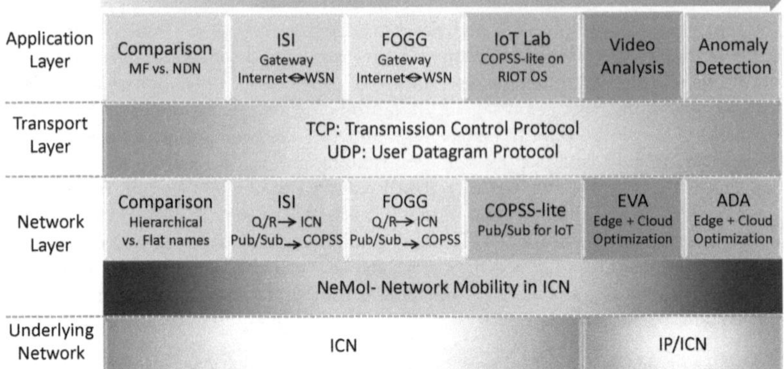

Figure 1.1: **Architecture of PHOENIX.**

1.3 book contributions

This book provides the following contributions to address the research prob-lems discussed in Section 1.2. In order to consolidate the contributions, this **book** also provides an architecture named PHOENIX: A Premise to Reinforce Heterogeneous and Evolving Internet Architectures with Exemplary Applications shown in Figure 1.1 that maps the contributions to their corresponding layers in the TCP/IP protocol suite [4].

1.3.1 Comparison of Naming Schema in ICN

To analyze the impact of naming schema and the resulting challenges that affect the performance of ICN networks (problem 1.2.1), we study the two most popular naming schemas among the ICN architectures — *hierarchical* names and *flat* names. Architectures like MF [2] and XIA [7] use (self-certifying) flat names whereas NDN [3, 6] adopts human-readable hierarchically structured names. The effectiveness of the network architectures using flat names and hierarchical names can be measured using a number of metrics: forwarding efficiency, aggregate-ability and semantics. However, in PHOENIX, we discovered that these metrics are interdependent. The forwarding efficiency might be affected by the lack of aggregate-ability since the size of the routing table can be large. Replication and mobility of content in the network can affect the aggregate-ability and increase the routing table size even with a hierarchical name space. The semantics and communication patterns can affect name space management and result in different table sizes. Therefore, a deeper study at the choice of these naming schemas is desirable, as this can be a key to the performance of ICN. To answer these questions, PHOENIX looks deeper into these metrics both qualitatively and quantitatively. In addition, the book tries to understand the *relationship* among these metrics and provides some hints for the choice of the optimal naming schema in ICN.

1.3.2 ISI: Integrate Sensor Networks to Internet with ICN

Even though the recent works like [46,47], *etc.* have focused on solving many different problems of IoT, they have not considered the crucial aspect of the need for an architecture to integrate the *SensorNetworks* running lighter version of ICN protocol with the Internet in order to realize IoT. Therefore, to address the problem of seamless integration of heterogeneous *Sensor Networks* to the Internet (problem 1.2.2), PHOENIX provides an architecture named ISI. Essentially, PHOENIX studies the various requirements for realizing an ICN based – IoT = Internet+SN architecture. Subsequently, PHOENIX proposes to introduce *Gateways* to integrate the *Sensor Networks* with the Internet. We identify the explicit functions, responsibilities and services of such a *Gateway* in an IoT environment. In addition, a suitable design for naming schema is provided to efficiently support the *Sensor Networks* operating with ICN protocols. Moreover, PHOENIX also analyzes the various communication patterns, mobility and security requirements of IoT devices to allow seamless communication across the heterogeneous networks.

1.3.3 Application - FOGG: A Fog Computing Based Gateway to Integrate Sensor Networks to Internet

Traditional Cloud based architectures direct user requests for storage and computing to nearby data centers. However, with increased focus towards low-latency and high bandwidth requirements form applications like high definition video streaming, technologies like Fog computing [13] have emerged. Fog computing is a promising new architecture that utilizes the multitude of end-user/edge-devices to carry out various operations like, storing, computing, controlling, *etc.* Fog computing can improve the QoS experienced by users through deploying the required storage at the edge of the network close to the users. Many applications, including but not limited to smart grids, sensor networks, industrial automation have been realized with Fog computing. Deployment of the future architectures like ICN can also greatly benefit with Fog computing as it expedites the process of integration with the existing technologies. In this work, exploit the benefits provided by Fog computing to connect the multitude of heterogeneous *Sensor Networks* to the Internet using the gateway designed in §1.3.2. This application studies the requirements for realizing such a Fog based – IoT = Internet+ SN design. Subsequently, *FOGG: A Fog Computing Based Gateway to Integrate Sensor Networks to Internet* is proposed. The primary focus of *FOGG* is to bridge the Internet (running on IP, ICN or other future protocols) with the IoT domains running ICN protocols. *FOGG* is designed to provide Fog based services such as name/protocol translation, security (secure onboarding), controller functionality and *etc.* and in this preliminary extension, the book focuses on a Fog based name/protocol translation service.

1.3.4 COPSS-lite: A Lightweight ICN based Pub/Sub System for IoT Environments

There are many recent works that focus on exploiting the features of CCN/NDN and COPSS for Internet and recent Interest towards supporting IoT environments with CCN/NDN. However, in PHOENIX we argue that IoT devices cannot support and does not need the full CCN/NDN stack. CCN-lite [20] is a recent effort by the research community towards producing a lightweight implementation for supporting IoT devices. However, like CCN/NDN, CCN-lite also faces the limitation to support efficient pub/sub features. Therefore, to address the need for a light-weight publish/subscribe system for IoT (problem 1.2.3) PHOENIX enhances the initial design of COPSS to provide *COPSS-lite: a Lightweight ICN based Pub/Sub system for IoT Environments*. Essentially, *COPSS-lite* implements the features of COPSS along with the IoT related enhancements with CCN-lite for enabling efficient pub/sub communication in the IoT environments.

1.3.5 NeMoI: Network Mobility in ICN

To address the network mobility in ICN (problem 1.2.4) PHOENIX proposes *NeMoI: Network mobility in ICN*, a comprehensive ICN based solution to support end-points that are within network-on-the-move. These end-points could be producers and/or consumers. Moreover, NeMoI is designed to seamlessly support the mobility of consumers and producers not located inside a moving network to avoid the need for multiple protocols for different scenarios. NeMoI also encompasses several optimization strategies that make it an efficient solution to support mobility in ICN. To the best of our knowledge, we believe that NeMoI is the first work to address network mobility in ICN. Through extensive evaluations on the RocketFuel1221 Telstra Australia [48] topology with 1M names PHOENIX shows that with NeMoI can reduce signalling traffic and routing updates from ~0.215B to ~4.6M in deterministic mobility scenario and 243,340 to 3,767 in non-deterministic mobility scenario. In addition, NeMoI also minimizes path inflation and packet loss in various scenarios and provides effective route optimization strategies.

1.3.6 Application - Network Mobility in Train and Car

In PHOENIX, we build deterministic and non-deterministic mobility scenarios using Train and Cars to evaluate the performance of NeMoI. Through a simulation of the RocketFuel AS1221 topology we construct realistic routes and study the effects of mobility and measure the benefits with NeMoI. Further, we also compare NeMoI with state-of-the-art approaches like, global updates, anchor-based and anchor-less based solutions. The evaluations show that, overall, NeMoI is dynamic and reactive to both micro and macro mobility. It also ensures reachability, reliability and connectivity during mobility and significantly improves the performance and user experience in ICN during mobility.

1.3.7 EVA: A Distributed Optimization Architecture for Efficient Video Analysis

To address the resource-accuracy optimization with supervised deep learning models (problem 1.2.5), PHOENIX proposes a 2-stage deep learning and rate adaption technique. This book proposes EVA: A Distributed Optimization Architec-ture for *E*fficient *V*ideo *A*nalysis which eliminates profiling and optimizes video analysis with a distributed architecture with the following characteristics:

- **No profiling:** We observed that, *Frame rate*, *resolution* and the number of layers in a DNN are the dominant metrics that influence the performance of video analysis [31]. Therefore, we propose a 2-stage deep learning process where we exploit the existing and newer incoming video data to train and build robust DNNs and eliminate the need for profiling. Specifically, we use Google's pre-trained InceptionV3 [42] Convolutional Neural Networks (CNN); These CNNs were trained on Imagenet's large visual recognition challenge dataset. We then use transfer learning to build efficient Recurrent Neural Networks (RNN) [49] with LSTM. Through exploiting the RNNs, we maintain the necessary temporal relationships among frames in a video during analysis and effectively identify events and actions; unlike current techniques which only use CNNs and thus, fail to acknowledge the temporal relationships among the frames and therefore can only analyze static images for identifying objects.

In 2-stage deep learning, during the first stage, termed as the "offline" stage we train and build DNNs by incrementally increasing the DNN layers until we obtain DNNs with high accuracy [50]. During the second stage termed as the "online" stage, we deploy these DNNs in their respective environment and continue training them with newer incoming videos in parallel to analyzing the videos.

- **Adaptive tuning:** We observed that, most of the suspicious/abnormal activities such as robbery, car accidents, *etc.*, are infrequent and occur for a very short duration in a video [51]. This insight formulated the desire in EVA to optimize and efficiently utilize the bandwidth and the scarce resources at the Edge. Therefore, we propose two rate adaption algorithms: Adaptive Frame Rate (AFR) and Adaptive Resolutions (ARR) to optimize the video analysis process to optimize the use of available computing resources and bandwidth.

- **Bandwidth reduction:** Through literature survey, we identified the minimal set of services in EVA for efficiently supporting VMS applications. Essentially, we propose a distributed architecture wherein the services [52] for caching, coding, video analysis and pub/sub are provided at the Edge while the long-term storage and streaming services are provided in the Cloud. Leveraging this distributed architecture, EVA efficiently steers the surveillance video traffic towards the Edge [53–56], and thereby alleviates it from consuming bandwidth in the core network [53]. In addition, EVA proposes to exploit the outcome of rate adaption during video analysis with AFR and ARR to efficiently utilize the available bandwidth in the first-hop to Edge in comparison to existing approaches as shown in our experiments in §10.2.

- **Storage cost reduction:** Incidentally, we also observed that since AFR and ARR can optimize the frame rate and resolution of the videos during analysis, they can also influence the frame rate and resolution at which these videos can be stored in the Edge and Cloud. As seen in our experiments (see §10.2), we greatly reduce the estimated storage cost [57–60] of the videos.

1.3.8 Application - Video Analysis

In PHOENIX, the performance EVA framework is measured with a video analysis application. We leverage the UCF-Crime dataset [61] and its corresponding ground-truth for normal and abnormal events like shoplifting to evaluate the benefits offered in EVA. Essentially, we measure the performance of the DNNs w.r.t. their prediction accuracy and latency during video analysis followed by comparing the proposed rate adaption algorithms: AFR and ARR with the recently proposed baseline profiling technique named Awstream from Zhang *et al.* [32]. Our evaluations show that,

AFR and ARR significantly outperform the state-of-the-art profiling approach and Awstream. Overall, we observe that, AFR improves the performance of the whole system by reducing the consumption of computational resources by 71% and latency of prediction by 69%; While, ARR reduces the consumption of computational resources by 36%, and latency of prediction by 56%. In comparison, the baseline profiling scheme Awstream, reduces the consumption of the computational resources by only 14% and latency by 13% when it profiled the videos at multiple frame rates and reduces consumption of computational resources by 9% and latency by 18% when it profiled the videos with different resolutions. Furthermore, the results also show that, with AFR we consumed 71% less bandwidth and 74% less storage whilst 61% less bandwidth and storage with ARR in comparison to Awstream which consumed 14% less storage and bandwidth when profiled at different frame rates and 21% less storage and 12% less bandwidth when profiled with different resolutions. We analyzed different rate adaption techniques [62] in AFR and ARR to select the optimal DNN. However, due to ease of understanding, we only show the best and least performing rate adaption techniques where we select the DNNs in an additive (best performance) and multiplicative fashion (least performance). We compare the rate adaption with Awstream and show that AFR and ARR outperform Awstream with not only their best rate adaption scheme but also with their least rate adaption technique. Moreover, we also compare the AFR and ARR algorithms and observe that AFR performs significantly better than ARR in all aspects (see §10.2). Hence, we deduce that AFR is a better candidate for current video analysis applications. However, with an increasing trend toward high-resolution video [63], ARR is suitable for improving the performance of many upcoming HD video analysis applications.

1.3.9 ADA: Adaptive Deep Log Anomaly Detector

To address the need for real-time security with unsupervised deep learning models (problem 1.2.6) PHOENIX provides *ADA: Adaptive Deep Log Anomaly Detector*, an efficient unsupervised online learning approach for detecting anomalies in system logs. Unlike recent works, we exploit the online deep learning [64] to build deep neural networks on the fly with LSTM using unlabelled log data collected from Los Alamos National Laboratory (LANL) Cyber Security Dataset [65]. Further, we also propose an adaptive prediction strategy where the pareto-optimal neural network configurations are selected for the current model from the set of all models obtained by online deep learning. In addition, since the patterns in log data are unstable, we develop a dynamic threshold algorithm which uses the recent predictions from the models to dynamically adapt the threshold for detecting abnormal events using the log-normal distribution. Utilizing adaptive strategy and dynamic threshold, ADA always selects the pareto-optimal neural network model with minimal configurations and current threshold based on system environment to predict every event in the system logs. The pareto-optimal policy first learns from the predictions obtained for earlier events. Then, it selects a model that optimizes the needed computational resources. The predictions also drive the decision for selectively storing the log data. Since we utilize the online deep learning, any system built using the ADA framework can effectively synchronize with any newly discovered log-patterns. Moreover, the system will use models with minimal configurations and predict anomalies with highest possible accuracy using optimal thresholds. To the best of our knowledge, we are first to propose online deep learning for detecting anomalies in log data with pareto-optimal models and dynamic thresholds.

1.3.10 Application - Cyber Security Data Analysis

In PHOENIX, we build an anomaly detection system based on the ADA framework and perform evaluations using the Los Alamos National Laboratory (LANL) Cyber Security Dataset [65] to measure the performance of ADA. Through extensive evaluation, PHOENIX shows that online deep learning produces highly accurate models where we obtain F1-scores in the range of 0.91 - 0.95 with the latency to predict in the range of 14 ms - 37 ms. We further observed that frequency of abnormal events are far less than normal events in the system logs, so we propose to store only abnormal events after prediction in order to optimally utilize the storage and reduce the overall storage cost.

1.4 book outline

The remainder of the book is organized as follows: in Chapter 2, a compre-hensive review of the background and relevant related research work is discussed. A comparison of the naming schema in ICN is presented in Chapter 3, followed by the architecture for integrating Sensor Networks to the Internet in Chapter 4 and an application of this architecture with Fog computing is presented in Chapter 5. Leveraging the publish/subscribe model for communication in IoT, the *COPSS-lite* architecture is presented in Chapter 6 and in Chapter 7, a proposal is made for enhancing the existing ICN architecture with network mobility followed by a perfor-mance evaluation of NeMoI with a deterministic (Train) and non-deterministic (Car) mobility application in Chapter 8. In Chapter 9, the framework EVA for optimizing resource-accuracy trade off with deep learning at Edge is presented followed by the performance evaluation of EVA with a video analysis application in Chapter 10. In Chapter 11, the framework ADA with adaptive method and dynamic threshold is presented to provide real-time security with unsupervised deep learning followed

by its performance evaluation with anomaly detection in system-logs in Chapter
12. Chapter 13 summarizes the book and provides future prospects and the impact
of the research performed in PHOENIX.

Chapter 2

Background and Related Work

This chapter initially introduces the fundamental concepts of ICN and pub/sub communication model to provide the necessary background knowledge for the contributions provided in the remainder of this book. A comprehensive study of the state-of-the-art research is then provided w.r.t. the open research problems ad-dressed in PHOENIX. The study mainly identifies the issues in the state-of-the-art approaches and reveals the need for the solutions provided in the book.

Contents

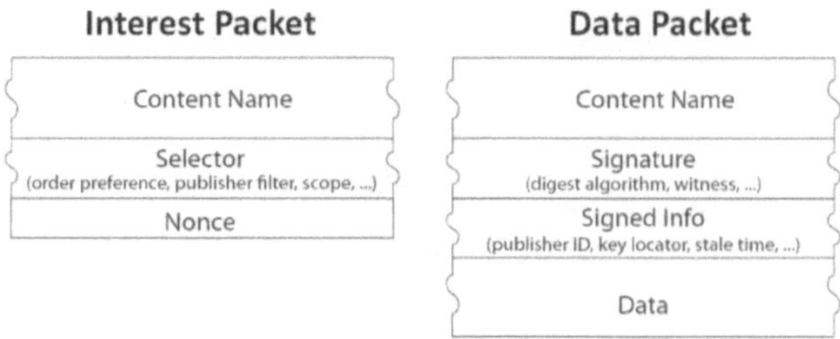

Figure 2.1: **CCN packet types** [1].

2.1 Background

ICN treats content as the first-class entity. It optimizes the data distribution and retrieval by integrating name resolution and routing in the network. Unlike IP, in ICN, nodes exchange information based on the identities of contents instead of the location. Each router in ICN can understand and decide where to forward the requests and hence, the network can find better sources for retrieving the content. This in turn reduces the latency and load on the network and content providers. In addition, ICN provides in-network caches which further optimizes the efficiency of the network due to its content awareness. ICN also enhances security by embedding the security in the content rather than on the communication link compared to IP. Moreover, ICN can easily support multicast and broadcast features for delivering the content to multiple users without additional overhead. In this section, we discuss the fundamentals of the representative ICN architectures used in PHOENIX.

2.1.1 NDN architecture

CCN also known as NDN [6] is the most popular ICN architecture to this date. It uses human-readable and hierarchically structured names similar to URLs as the *content name*. In NDN, producers of the content announce prefixes of their sources globally to advertise the content. To deliver the data efficiently, NDN introduces two new packets for query/response: *Interest* (*i.e.*, request) and *Data* (*i.e.*, content) shown in Figure 2.1. The CCN forwarding engine model used for data delivery is shown in Figure 2.2. Every router uses the three data structures from the forwarding engine model as follows: *1) Forwarding Information Base (FIB)*: stores content names and their outgoing faces. *2) Pending Interest Table (PIT)*: stores all the pending Interests and their incoming faces. *3) Content Store (CS)*: caches the content received from upstream.

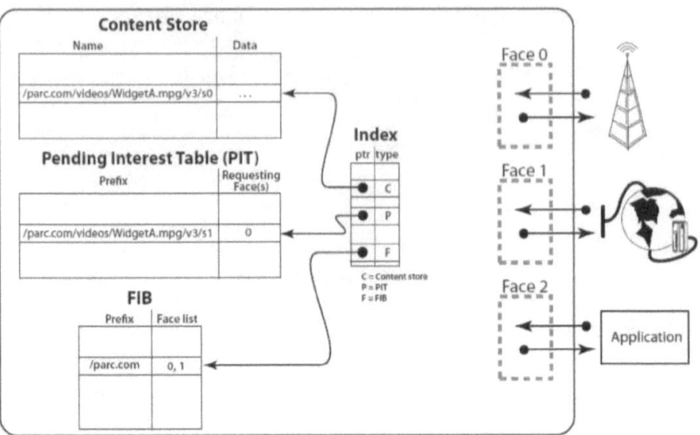

Figure 2.2: **CCN forwarding engine model** [1].

The NDN communication protocol usually begins when a user generates an Interest with the *content name*. The Interest is satisfied either by the producer or any intermediate node in the network with a copy of the content. When the Interest arrives at a CCN router, CS in the forwarding engine of the router is checked to see if the content with the same name already exists, in which case the content is returned to the user. In case of a CS miss, the PIT is checked to see if an Interest with the same name has already been forwarded upstream in the network. If yes, then the incoming face of the Interest is recorded in the PIT. If not, an entry is added to the PIT with the *content name* and incoming face. The FIB is then queried to find the forwarding face (next hop) and the Interest is forwarded to the next hop router. Similarly, when a Data packet arrives at a router, the CS is checked, and if a matching entry is present then the Data packet is discarded (as it is an unsolicited content) otherwise, the CS stores the Data and PIT is checked. If an entry is found in the PIT then the Data is forwarded to all the incoming faces recorded in the PIT for this *content name*. Otherwise the Data packet is discarded.

2.1.2 MobilityFirst architecture

Mobility First (MF) [2] is a recently proposed ICN architecture (shown in Figure 2.3) which tries to optimize the performance when the mobile devices are the majority in the network. Each entity, either a device, an application, or a content is assigned

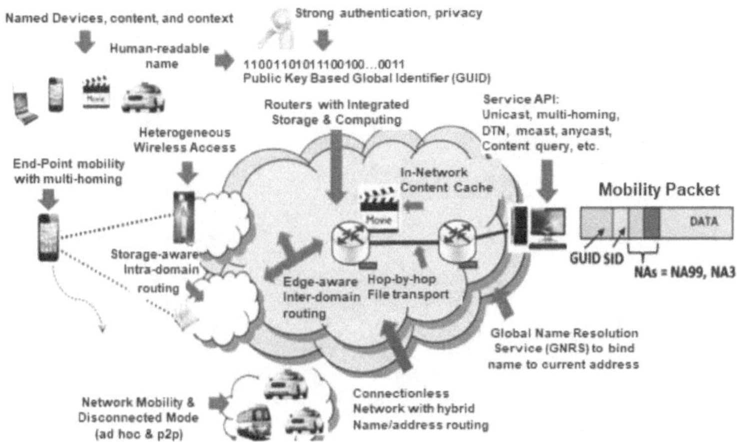

Figure 2.3: **MobilityFirst architecture [2].**

a 20-byte flat Globally Unique IDentifier (GUID) which is essentially a public key assigned by a Name Certification Service (NCS). The GUIDs have no relationship with their Network Address (NA). The key component of the MF architecture is a name resolution service called the Global Name Resolution Service (GNRS). It is a distributed *network layer* service adopted to maintain the dynamic relationship between GUID and NA(s). Different from DNS, the query for a NA is sent by the routers instead of the sender (late binding). During forwarding any intermediate router can query the GNRS to get the current NA mapping(s) to enable dynamic binding of the GUID to the NA(s) during mobility. Thereby, the MF routers can easily redirect a packet locally to the destination. Similar to NDN, MF also uses in-network caching when possible and establishes trust and security by leveraging self-certifying names.

The communication protocol in MF for exchanging data can begin after the assignment of GUID from a NCS. Once, the GUIDs are assigned, a user A who wishes to send data to another user B will first obtains the GUID of B from either a NCS service are directly from B. The user A then invokes the MF service API through a command like (GUID, option, data) where the option can indicate the type of data delivery service like, multi-cast, broadcast or anycast. The user A's host computer then generates the MF packet (shown in Figure 2.3) and queries the GNRS with the GUID to get the corresponding NA to forward the packet. The GNRS

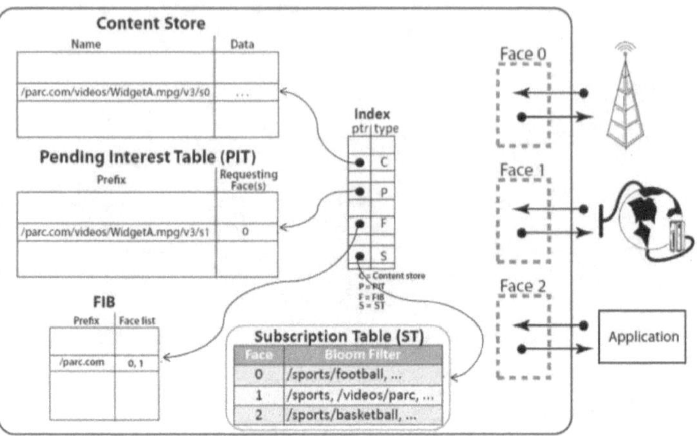

Figure 2.4: **CCN forwarding engine model [1] with COPSS [3] subscription table.**

lookup returns the current set of NAs which represents the point of attachment in the network. The NA are added to the packet by the host computer and forwarded in the network. Each router in the network uses the NA in the packet to find the next-hop router to forward the packet. When a packet delivery fails due to mobility, the respective intermediate router queries the GNRS to get the current set of NAs to account for mobility. The packet is eventually delivered to the user B.

2.1.3 COPSS architecture

COPSS drew special attention to the popular pub/sub systems running over IP in the Internet through studying the additional responsibility/burden that is incurred with the IP based solutions. In [66, 67] authors show that IP based pub/sub solutions tend to waste network resources. Similarly, COPSS identified the shortcoming of NDN to support pub/sub in an ICN environment. In principle, NDN requires the subscribers to either know the publisher or the precise name of the published content. However, this is not a mandatory requirement in pub/sub environment; as they wish to eliminate temporal dependency. Thus, NDN fails to support this fundamental requirement. Hence, a Content-Oriented Pub/Sub System (COPSS) [3] was proposed by Chen *et al.* to enhance the initial design of CCN by integrating it with an efficient and scalable pub/sub capability. COPSS based its pub/sub architecture on utilizing the concept of Content Descriptors (CD). In general, CD's

Subscription

Content Descriptors
Selector (order preference, publisher filter, scope, ..)
Nonce

Publication

Content Name
Content Descriptors
Signature (digest algorithm, witness, ...)
Signed Info (publisher ID, key locator, stale time, ...)
Data

Figure 2.5: **COPSS packet types [3].**

can be described as the features that can represent the content like keywords, date of publication, identity of the publisher, *etc.* Further, COPSS also expanded the scope of CD's to support ontologies, content hierarchies and context based content identification.

In principal, COPSS adds a Subscription Table (ST) to the initial CCN forwarding engine shown in Figure 2.4. Every COPSS router maintains the ST for enabling pub/sub in a distributed and aggregated manner. COPSS also introduces two new packets shown in Figure 2.5: *Subscribe* and *Publish.* The Subscribe packet is used by the users to subscribe to a certain CD while the Publish packet is used by the publisher to publish content for a single or group of CD's *i.e.*, a piece of content can be associated with multiple CD's. Each CD is assigned to a respective Rendezvous Point (RP) node in the network. Subscribers can subscribe to the content of their interest by subscribing to the associated CD's, resulting in a join. When a router receives a subscription request, it adds an entry in its ST with the CD and the incoming face of the request before forwarding the request upstream. The subscription request is forwarded towards the RP with each intermediate router adding an entry for the subscription in their ST. When the publisher generates any content, she/he associates the content with the relevant CDs. Whenever the content is published, it travels along the multicast tree towards the responsible RP and then downstream to towards the subscribers. When a router receives a publication packet, it checks the ST for any one of the CD's in the publication packet. If a match is found then the router forwards the publication along the matched interfaces. However, only a single copy of the publication is forwarded on each interface, irrespective of the number of subscribers downstream. This avoids, unnecessary traffic and duplicate/-multiple copies delivered to the subscribers of more than one CD in the publication. In addition, COPSS also provides a two-step communication process which allows the publishers to exercise control over the access and policy of the published contents. In a two-step communication process, the publishers generate a snippet of the original content with the associated CD's and send it to the subscribers. Interested subscribers can then use these CD's to subscribe to the full-length original content. The publishers then publish the original content which is forwarded to the interested subscribers as explained earlier.

2.2 Related work

2.2.1 Impact of naming schema on the performance of ICN

With the proposals of different ICN solutions, there are also many comparisons to show the benefits and issues with each solution. They can be generally classified into 3 categories: *1) compare the different design choices of each solution 2) evaluate each design choice with different applications* and *3) look at a specific module in the solution.*

Bari *et al.* [68] performs a qualitative comparison of naming and routing mechanisms in various ICN architectures. It compares security and data integrity in flat *vs.* hierarchical names and suggests a multilayer naming scheme. It also compares the in-path *vs.* off-path name resolution and provides a list of desired properties for routing in ICN. Ahlgren *et al.* [69] compares the basics of several ICN architectures with a main focus on the choices these architectures make for naming, security, routing, transport, caching and API.

Work in [70,71] compares NDN and MF with different applications. In [70] applications like content retrieval, unicast and mobility are compared and observations reveal that MF scales better than CCN and [71] builds an architecture for IoT in NDN and MF and compares them for service discovery and pub/sub models by measuring delay, throughput and control overhead. Observation reveal that MF incurs less overhead in terms of routing table size and control messages.

Work in [72,73] compares several modules in various ICN architectures. In [72] modules like FIB size, path stretch and cost of routing updates are assessed quantitatively revealing that mobility affects routing updates in ICN. In [73] NDN and HTTP are compared with the level of caches and number of clients as metrics revealing that CCNx is 10 times slower than HTTP.

We find that none of the aforementioned works examine the choice of naming schema — a fundamental design choice that can affect and be affected by all the other components and use cases — in depth. The choice of naming schema draws the boundary between the application layer and the network layer, and different choices implicitly result in different functionality separations. Therefore, in PHOENIX, we focus on the naming schema alone in Chapter 3 and try to understand how the various components are interlinked and their impact on the choice of naming schema in ICN.

2.2.2 IoT: seamless integration of heterogeneous *Sensor Networks* to the Internet

The relevant recent works that focus on leveraging ICN for IoT and compute environments can be broadly classified into the following five categories:

2.2.2.1 Architecture

Authors in [46] propose an initial high-level design for IoT using NDN architecture. It divides the NDN layer into two planes: data plane and management & control plane. The data plane handles query/response while the control plane re-engineers the current NDN routing plane. In [19], authors analyze the current TCP/IP solutions for supporting IoT. They argue that existing TCP/IP solutions are inefficient and propose that IoT can benefit by using ICN. In [74], authors experiment with two ICN architectures namely, MF and NDN for IoT environment. They name these architectures MF-IoT and NDN-IoT and compare their performance. Whereas in [75], authors propose to use ICN for IoT to realize service oriented communication. They use MF as an example ICN architecture and modify it to support the service oriented communication in IoT.

2.2.2.2 Routing/Caching

Authors in [47] discuss the shortcomings of CCN protocol for IoT and propose a routing protocol with a complexity of O(1) and almost no control traffic. They exploit the caching and data path in ICN to support the IoT requirements. They also show that CCN-lite uses 80% less memory compared to IP. Whereas in [76], authors study the benefit of caching with ICN for IoT in terms of energy consumption and bandwidth utilization in comparison with IP.

2.2.2.3 Protocol

Authors in [77] focus on a specific type of data retrieval pattern called multi-source data retrieval. They argue that current NDN architecture does not support this type of communication and propose a solution where consumers use multi-source Interest to retrieve data from multiple producers. They also propose to delete the PIT entry based on Interest life time (*i.e.*, TTL) instead of deleting when the data is received the first time. Whereas in [78], authors study the potential for using ICN based solutions for Wireless Sensor Area Networks (WSAN) and discuss how ICN for WSAN is different from ICN for Internet. Essentially, they use flat names and continuous Interest to receive data sensed by multiple sensors; as multiple sensors in WSAN sense the same data and respond to the Interest.

2.2.2.4 Securtiy

Authors in [79] propose a protocol for authenticating and authorizing new devices joining the IoT mesh networks in ICN. They show 87% improvement in communication and 66% improvement in energy consumption compared ZigBee and IP based solutions. While authors in [80] compare two approaches based on Asymmetric and Symmetric key encryptions for deploying new IoT devices in existing ICN deployments. They report that although the Asymmetric key based solutions incur lower traffic they impose higher demands on energy and time consumption.

2.2.2.5 Computing in ICN

In [81], authors show that Cloud computing needs a stable infrastructure and networking. They explore the ICN protocol NetInf [82] for supporting networking and storage in the Cloud. They analyze the benefits that could be offered to Cloud computing environments through utilizing a name based networking infrastructure especially for management, storage and deployment in dynamic networking environments. While Authors in [83] show that with the increased amount of information exchange in modern day devices, Fog computing and ICN can help in managing the Cloud environment. They propose a framework with ICN as an API for ubiquitous computing and leverage the caching from ICN and utilize Fog computing with names instead of IP addresses. The authors in [84] explore Fog computing for supporting IoT applications and services. While, authors in [85] discuss the need for edge computing with the increasing popularity of IoT and Cloud services. Whereas in [86], authors propose the architecture NetFATE to place VNF at the edge of the network.

The above mentioned related works propose to leverage the benefits of either Edge/Fog or ICN or both for supporting IoT networks; however, they fail to account for the heterogeneity of the *Sensor Networks* and the need for seamless integration of *Sensor Networks* for efficient data delivery. Similar to the recent works, in Chapter 4&5 we exploit the benefits of ICN and Fog computing to support the IoT networks. However, we also provide an avenue to connect the heterogeneous *Sensor Networks* to the Internet to realize IoT through a dedicated Gateway with improved functionality.

2.2.3 Light-weight publish/subscribe system for IoT

While several ICN frameworks like NDN [6], MF [2], XIA [7], PSIRP [87] have been proposed for the Internet, they cannot directly be employed in an IoT environment due to constrained device requirements. The relevant recent works that focus on leveraging ICN to support IoT environment are discussed below:

Many recent works that propose to use ICN for IoT focus on major areas like data retrieval patterns [77], routing [47], benefits of caching [76], security [88], disaster relief [89] and architectural changes [46]. While [90] provides a comprehensive review of the data delivery mechanisms in the ICN environment. In [91], authors perform experiments with NDN in an IoT environment to identify the feasibility and challenges of ICN for supporting IoT environment. They perform an indoor experiment with numerous NDN enabled IoT devices and identify the shortcomings of ICN for IoT like data freshness *vs.* caching and overhead of in-network forwarding. While authors in [92] utilize the ICN slicing framework to build services at the Edge for IoT. In [93], authors propose a protocol named MobCCN which creates opportunistic content-centric networks for IoT devices to access nearby data whereas in [94], authors create opportunistic context-virtual networks to create virtual groups of interested nodes in a network to optimize the resource utilization. Authors in [95, 96] propose ICN based architectures for IoT environments. In [95] authors propose an overlay ICN architecture for M2M communication in IoT, while in [96] authors identify the high-level requirements and ICN based architecture for IoT. Whereas in [88] authors propose attribute based encryption for providing security in resource constrained environments and in [97] authors provide a convergence layer with NDN for 6LoWPAN along with compression schemes.

In [98] authors devise a proposal to use NDN in mobile ad hoc network (MANET) scenarios and in [99] authors evaluate the MANETS in IP and NDN while in [100], authors use NDN and Bluetooth Low Energy (BLE) in constrained environments to enable robust communications to reuse existing BLE applications. In [101, 102] authors propose to push the data in ICN. In [101], authors use sampling optimization to reduce the traffic and propose to ask the produces to add the data inside the Interest packet and forward it to the destination without storing the Interest in the routers PIT and further disable the caching. In [102], authors propose a pub/sub mechanism for IoT, but use IP as the underlay instead of ICN. Whereas in, CCN-lite [20] authors provide an inter-operable implementation of the CCNx and NDN protocol to support IoT.

The above mentioned recent works propse to exploit the features of ICN (and IP) for supporting efficient communication in IoT environments. However, they leverage the standard CCN/NDN representation and hence they lack support for an efficient pub/sub communication model which is an essential requirement in the IoT environments. Even though COPSS enhances NDN with pub/sub, there is still a need for a lighter version of COPSS for supporting pub/sup in the IoT networks. Therefore, in PHOENIX, we provide a lighter implementation of COPSS named *COPSS-lite* in Chapter 6 for enabling pub/sub based communication in the IoT environments.

2.2.4 Network mobility in ICN

ICN inherently supports consumer mobility. However, producer mobility on the other hand is still an open issue. In CCN, since routers in the network maintain information about how to reach the producers/sources, whenever a producer moves to a new location, every router in the network requires an update. In the meantime, the network is incapable of satisfying any requests until the mobility updates are propagated in the network. Hence, we studied the relevant producer mobility literature and broadly classified them into the following four categories:

2.2.4.1 Anchors

In anchor based methods, a dedicated anchor is used to manage the mobility of the producers. A mobile producer notifies the anchor whenever it changes its point of attachment in the network. The request for content are re-directed to the anchor which then forwards it to the current location of the mobile producer. Mobile IP [26] and ICN solutions like Lee *et al.* [103] use such anchor based approaches to handle mobility. Essentially a tunnel is established between the Home Access Router (HAR) of the mobile producer and the Foreign Access Router (FAR) where the producer currently resides. When the producer moves, the requests are redirected towards the HAR which encapsulates the packets and forwards it to the producer. In [22], authors proposed a solution similar to an actual Kite to support producer mobility. Essentially, when producers move, they notify a dedicated immobile anchor about their new location using a Traced *Interest*. The Traced *Interest* is not deleted from the PIT and will be used to forward the *Interests* towards the current location of the producers.

Anchor based solutions are reactive in nature and have minimal service interruption time. However, they increase the signalling traffic and induce path stretch in the network. Moreover, tunneling changes the *content name* and hence, affects the caching and aggregation in ICN.

2.2.4.2 Anchorless

In anchorless methods, every mobile node is responsible to notify the network about its mobility related information. In [21], authors use *Interest* Update (IU) and Temporary FIB (TFIB) to propagate the mobility updates. The producers send IU to their previous point of attachment whenever there is a change in their physical location due to mobility. The intermediate routers that forward the IU also update their TFIB. Similarly, authors in [104,105] also propose anchorless based approaches for supporting mobility in ICN.

Anchorless solutions are more reactive compared to anchor based solutions and also support frequent location changes. However, they also incur path stretch and signalling traffic as producers generate update for every prefix during mobility.

2.2.4.3 Resolution

In resolution based methods, several dedicated nodes in the network resolve the names to their respective current locations. In IP, the traditional DNS is used to resolve URL's to their respective IP addresses which are subsequently used to reach the producers. However, mobility in IP results in a new IP address. In LISP [106], an additional resolution step is needed to resolve the identifiers to locators. In MF [2], a 20-bit GUID is assigned to every entity and a distributed resolution architecture is used to resolve the GUIDs to the current location of the users. In [23], authors proposed *OPRA* where they place route resolvers at multiple points on the path to a content for reaching the source.

The resolution based approaches scale well and also produce less signalling traffic compared to anchor and anchorless based approaches. However, they also incur path stretch and hence, they are not suitable for supporting frequent mobility scenarios especially, for latency-sensitive applications.

2.2.4.4 Locator/Identifier split

Many solutions like [27,106] propose to separate locator from Identifer. They use an immobile anchor in the home domain but unlike Mobile IP, they do not use encapsulation. The anchor receives *Interest*s on behalf of the producer and generates a new *Interest* with the name of the mobile producer at the new location and sends the content back to the consumer. Upon receiving the content the Anchor sends the content to the consumer. Whereas in [107], authors propose a service driven architecture where mobility is an on-demand service provided by the network.

They leverage the ID/Locator split to maintain persistent names and avoid name reconfiguration due to mobility

The locator/identifier split based solutions include topology dependant information in the name or in the payload. However, mobility changes the locator and hence, such solutions will also result in changing the content object.

Overall, many of the above mentioned solutions address only static producer mobility (i.e., nodes move from one point to another and remain there for a considerable time period [21]). Moreover, the IP based network mobility solutions cannot be directly adopted in ICN. Therefore, in **PHOENIX** we provide a comprehensive solution named NeMoI in Chapter 7 to support mobile end points and end points in network-on-the-move.

2.2.5 Resource-accuracy optimization with supervised deep learning models

We studied the relevant recent works that focus on optimizing the performance of video analysis applications with deep learning to achieve desired resource-accuracy trade off and broadly classifying them into the following two categories:

2.2.5.1 Video analysis

Chen *et al.* [29] investigate computing platforms for high-performance applications and show that video surveillance is a widely used and very resource demanding application. Similarly, Karimaa *et al.* [108], through an analysis of dependability characteristics of video surveillance and safety-critical applications like: availability, security, reliability and maintainability, provide insight for moving video surveillance from traditional systems to Cloud based systems. While Hamida *et al.* [109] study the effects of scalability with increasing number of surveillance cameras and propose a scalable framework with spatio-temporal filtering. Kumar *et al.* [63] highlight the increasing demand for high-performance video surveillance algorithms due to increasing popularity of HD videos and Feng *et al.* [110] identify the challenges for hosting large-scale video analysis applications for a futuristic artificially intelligent city and propose a framework for anomaly detection.

The above mentioned recent works focus mainly on additional functionalities like profiling, filtering, parallelization, *etc.*, to improve the performance of video anaylsis. However, such operations induce overhead and consume additional resources beside the resources required by video analysis algorithms. Therefore, in **PHOENIX** we

provide a solution named EVA in Chapter 9 where we study the current limitations
of video analysis and its effect on response time. Unlike the recent works, we take a
different approach by leveraging the accuracy of prediction during video analysis as
a feedback to optimize the resource-accuracy trade off and improve the performance
of video analysis algorithms.

2.2.5.2 Profiling

Mcdnn [28], Noscope [111] and Focus [112] train specialized DNNs to improve the
accuracy of detection during video analysis. Similarly, authors in [30, 31] try to
improve the performance of video analysis by profiling the configurations such as
DNN layers, frame rate, *etc.* However, these solutions depend on initial profiling to
improve the accuracy and do not change configurations during analysis to account
for changing content in the video during analysis. Therefore, these solutions cannot
be used to improve the performance during analysis. Jiang *et al.* [14] presens a
profiler to dynamically choose the best configurations for improving DNN based
analytic's performance. While, Zhang *et al.* [32] propose Awstream which uses a
generalized API with maybe operators to dynamically fine-tune application knobs
during profiling to match application's data-rate to the bandwidth.

Although, dynamic profiling in [14, 32] can improve the performance during analysis, they still focus on mainly optimizing profiling to improve the performance.
However, Zhang *et al.* [32] show that profiling adds additional overhead and demands increased computational resources in addition to the resources required by
DNNs during video analysis [32]. Hence, unlike the above mentioned recent works,
in EVA, we propose to eliminate the overhead of profiling during video analysis. In
summary, we propose a 2-stage deep learning technique with rate adaption to achieve
the desired resource-accuracy trade off with DNNs during video analysis.

2.2.6 Real-time security with unsupervised deep learning models

We studied the relevant recent works that focus on improving security through
anomaly detection in system-logs with deep learning and broadly classify them into
the following three categories:

2.2.6.1 Rule-based approaches

Many recent works such as [113–116] use rule-based approaches to detect anomalies.
Rule-based approaches tend to detect anomalies with great accuracies. However,

they depend heavily on expert domain knowledge and hence they cannot be generalized to detect logs from multiple different systems. Moreover, employing experts to build rules is expensive, labor intensive and time consuming.

2.2.6.2 Supervised learning approaches

Supervised learning techniques like [38, 39, 117, 118] have been widely explored for network anomaly detection. For example, [38] employs a tree model based on the random forest method to detect anomalies in the data in crowd sourced networks. In these methods, both normal and abnormal vectors are required to train a binary classifier to detect future anomalies. The main disadvantage of such approaches is that they heavily depend on an experts' experience to label the log data. However, even for an expert it is challenging to distinguish and define anomalies. In addition such operations are often expensive and labor intensive. Another downside of such approaches is there inability to detect newer anomalies that were not part of the training data.

2.2.6.3 Unsupervised learning approaches

Du et al. [36] propose an online log anomaly detector where customized parsing methods are employed on the logs to generate sequences for LSTM or clustering algorithms to detect DoS attacks. However they require pre-define and customized parsing methods for detection. In [43, 119] authors employ RNN and LSTM attention algorithms to improve the performance of anomaly detection in logs. However, they are defined from a user's perspective, where each user's behaviour is trained on a separate LSTM network and hence the number of LSTM networks increases with the increase in the number of users over time. Mirsky et al. [120] present the kitsune framework by using an ensembles of autoencoders for network anomaly detection. However, kitsune adds a separate feature extraction step which requires a basic understanding of the underlying network protocols. In [41], authors use adversarial training of VAE to detect anomalies in key performance monitors of the network however, it unsuitable for online systems as the adversarial training is unstable and difficult to converge. Khatuya et al. [121] propose ADELE, with an aim to select features from system logs in order to create groundwork for a proactive, online failure prediction system. However, this system can perform only short-term failure predictions in the current environment. Moreover, it needs to be trained for at least a month to compute the anomaly score. Authors from [122] highlight that, anomaly detection is time sensitive and decisions have to be made in streaming fashion. This enables the system administrators to intervene in an on-going attack or fix a system performance issue. In this regard, offline learning strategies like [38, 41, 44, 117],

that require the knowledge of prior pattern of normal and abnormal events are
not suitable for the new detection systems and also for existing systems trained on
outdated events.

Unlike the aforementioned recent works, in PHOENIX we propose an efficient
framework named ADA in Chapter 11 to build efficient real-time anomaly detection
systems using unsupervised online deep learning. By leveraging the adaptive strategy ADA computes thresholds dynamically to improve the F1-score and accuracy of
anomaly detection. In addition the proposed framework further reduces the latency
during analysis and improves the storage requirements of the system log data.

Chapter 3

Comparison of Naming Schema in ICN

ICN treats content as a first-class entity — each content has a unique identity and ICN routers forward traffic based on content identity rather than the locations of the content. This provides benefits like dynamic request routing, caching and mobility support. The choice of naming schema (flat *vs.* hierarchical) is a fundamental design choice in ICN which determines the functional separation between the network layer and the application layer. With hierarchical names, the network layer is cognizant of the semantics of hierarchical names. Name space management is also part of network layer. ICN architectures using flat names leave these to the application layer. The naming schema affects the performance and scalability of the network in terms of forwarding efficiency, routing table size and name space size. This chapter provides both qualitative and quantitative comparison on the two naming schemas using these metrics, noting that they are *interdependent*. We seek to understand which naming schema would be better for a high-performance, scalable ICN architecture.

The key contributions in this work include:

- We start with the basic metric — the forwarding efficiency with hierarchical *vs.* flat names. The forwarding engine of NDN and the Global Name Resolution Service (GNRS) of MF are benchmarked in this evaluation.
- The FIB size is then studied *under the assumption of data movement/replication*. The aggregate-ability of hierarchical names is evaluated with a million content names, with realistic mobility of the content in a real-world topology.
- The size of the name space is further examined *in different application semantics and name space manageability* to show the benefits and costs of using hierarchical *vs.* flat names.
- Based on the evaluations, we provide our observation and thoughts on hierarchical *vs.* flat names.

Contents

3.1 Comparison 1: name lookup efficiency

We start our comparison with the key metric in the network for performance —
forwarding efficiency. Forwarding performance affects throughput and latency of
the network, especially in the backbone. If we abstract routers (forwarding engines)
as an object containing multiple (routing) tables, the efficiency of lookups is key.

Since ICN uses the identity (name) of the content as the routing label, routers
have to lookup and manage the routing tables based on names as well. In NDN,
each *content name* is formed by multiple components connected using "/", similar to
URLs in the current Internet. Since there is no bound on the length of each component, or the number of components, content names can be of arbitrary length which
makes the existing hardware optimizations for fixed-length lookups ineffective [123].
For flat names, solutions like MF use constant length (20-byte) strings as content
identifiers (GUIDs). Therefore, the name table lookup is equal to a (distributed)
hash table lookup and can result in relatively small lookup time.

3.1.1 Microbenchmark: NDN forwarding *vs.* MF GNRS

To better understand the lookup efficiency of hierarchical *vs.* flat names, we first
perform measurements, to obtain a microbenchmark on the data structure used by
the NDN (CCNx) forwarding engine and the GNRS in MF.

We acknowledge that the utility of these two entities are not equivalent — the
NDN forwarding engine performs on-path name resolution while GNRS does it off-
path. However the functionality of the two entities are similar — name resolution.

We believe that this comparison is useful for both architectures: it can shed some light on the performance of the NDN forwarding engine if it uses flat names (similar to GNRS) and the performance of GNRS if it uses hierarchical names.

We also realize that the performance in CCNx implementation is affected by the use of locks and the pull model in socket programming. The pull-based implementation is efficient when there are a lot of packets going through the forwarding engine since less time will be wasted for context switching between the kernel and user. However, the implementation makes it difficult for us to study the lookup efficiency in isolation. To make a fair comparison, we use an alternative implementation in the CCNx Java version, called `InterestTable`. It provides `add` and `getMatch` function, similar to the FIB.

For populating the data structures, we take the top 1M websites ranked by the Alexa.com [124] based on average traffic in November 2015 as the data set of names. Since the original names are in the form of domain names (*e.g.*, `commsec.com.au`), to translate them into the NDN format, we reverse the domain name components and join them with a "/" (*e.g.*, the name would become `/au/com/commsec`). For flat names, MD5 hash is directly used as *content name.*

We observe that the lookup efficiency in both NDN and MF is affected by the size of FIB. Therefore, we measure the lookup time with different FIB sizes ranging from 0.1, 0.2 to 1M. For each FIB size, we perform 1M random lookups among the names already inserted and get the average latency with 95% confidential interval. The results are shown in Figure 3.1. We can see that with flat names, GNRS implementation achieves much lower lookup latency (within 1.5ms) compared to InterestTable. The lookup time with flat names shows a logarithmic growth *vs.* FIB size while hierarchical name solution has a linear increase with the FIB size.

We acknowledge that results may vary with implementation, name structure and hardware. However, we argue that for hierarchical names, the time used to decode the name components and find proper entries in the name tree (LPM) is inevitably more complex compared to flat name lookup. Moreover, flat names can be easily compressed by data structures like BloomFilters without losing lookup efficiency, but it is not easy to do the same thing in a hierarchical name tree.

3.1.2 Discussion

In addition to the benchmarked implementations, there are other solutions that have sought to accelerate the lookup speed for hierarchical names. *E.g.*, work in [125] tries to use GPU to perform the lookup at line speed and So *et al.* [] use

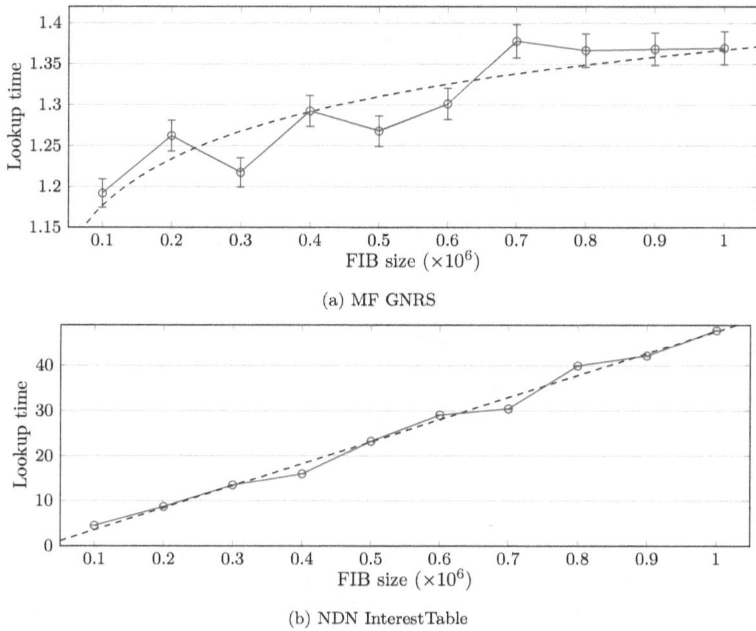

(a) MF GNRS

(b) NDN InterestTable

Figure 3.1: Lookup time (ms) vs. FIB size on MF vs. NDN.

2 Xeon processors (24-logical cores) to achieve 20Gbps forwarding speed. Interestingly, neither one of these implementation follow the original name hierarchy within the network. The GPU solution breaks names into 3-strides (*e.g.*, break /com/yahoo/www into com, /, yah, oo/ and www) noting that "3" is the maximum size of the stride that can be supported in the GPU memory (3GB). Similarly, the CPU (Xeon) solution computes the hash of the *full* name before it performs the lookup in the FIB. In these solutions, it is very difficult to examine the semantics of hierarchical names in the network (*e.g.*, find the latest version of a file) since they treat them as flat names. From these implementations, we can see that the bounded flat name space is preferred by hardware implementations to achieve high-speed lookup. Nonetheless, with either flat or hierarchical names, the size of the FIB is still the key factor in routing table management and lookup efficiency. When the routing table becomes too large, distributed solutions will inevitably be used to make the table management feasible, but this increases the memory consumption (redundancy) and the time for lookup (communication latency).

37

3.2 Comparison 2: aggregate-ability

To reduce the size of FIB, solutions with hierarchical names can aggregate based
on the name hierarchy similar to IP. *E.g.*, on a router (R), if all the names under /sports (/sports/ football, /sports/basketball, ...) are served on a
same outgoing (inter)face (f), R can aggregate these names as only *one* FIB entry: {/sports $\mapsto f$}. These solutions will also use *longest prefix matching* (LPM)
for the name lookup. On seeing a request with name /sports/football/ games,
the FIB would forward the request towards f since /sports is the longest prefix
match. If there is another entry {/sports/football $\mapsto f'$}, the same name will be
forwarded to face f' since the new entry becomes the LPM.

Such solutions have performed well in IP network since the address space is assigned by network managers. In the routing table, one entry can be used to represent
a large address space, *e.g.*, 134.76.0.0/16 $\mapsto f$. However, in ICN, the name of the
content is usually not assigned by the network provider. Even if the content follows
the domain hierarchy like IP *when it is created*, such a systematic allocation can be
easily violated by data mobility and/or replication. Cisco [126] predicts that WiFi
and mobile devices will account for 61 percent of network traffic by 2016. When a
mobile device with content moves from one domain to another, it is very difficult
to rename each *content name* in that device. Data replication (especially through
caching) has the potential to reduce the load on the network and content provider.
It is one of the major benefits provided by ICN. When the data is replicated in another domain, changing it to another name with the domain prefix would diminish
the benefits of naming the content to achieve aggregate-ability. The potential of
achieving a smaller FIB size with hierarchical names is thus conflicted by the fact
that the names are no longer easily aggregate-able.

3.2.1 Simulation: name aggregation on content mobility

To study the effect of data mobility on the FIB size, we perform a simulation on a
real world topology (RocketFuel1221, Telstra, Australia [48]) with the same name
data set studied in §3.1. According to [48], Telstra has hubs in major cities (Sydney,
Melbourne, Perth, *etc.*) with spokes elsewhere. To make the topology more like a
typical customer edge/provider network, with customer edge networks multi-homed,
we added several links between the spoke cities and the routers at their original hub
compared to the aggregate representation in [48].

We use the "hub" cities as first-level domains (*e.g.*, Sydney would have domain prefix /Sydney) and the "spoke" cities as second-level domains (*e.g.*, New-

Table 3.1: **Different aggregation algorithms can yield different FIB size. Example of /a, /b, /c going to f_1 and /d going to f_2, both FIB can get the correct result with LPM.**

(a) FIB aggregation 1

Prefix	Outgoing Face
/	f_1
/n4	f_2
—	—
—	—

(b) FIB aggregation 2

Prefix	Outgoing Face
/	f_2
/n1	f_1
/n2	f_1
/n3	f_1

castle, which has links only to Sydney, would have domain prefix /Sydney/ Newcastle). Each router in the topology has a unique sub name space in the form of /CityPrefix/RouterPrefix (*e.g.*, router "Sydney,+Australia4208" uses prefix /Sydney/ 4208 and router "Newcastle,+Australia 3930" uses prefix /Sydney/Newcastle/3930).

At the beginning of the evaluation, we place the 1M names randomly on each router and rename them using the form /RouterPrefix/Name (*e.g.*, /com/google is placed on Sydney 4208 router and it is renamed as /Sydney/4208/ com/google). To study the effect of data replication on aggregate-ability of hierarchical names, we start to replicate the names into other domains *while keeping the original name*. The FIB size is measured at each replication percentage from 10%, 20% to 200% (in which case, each name has 2 replicas in some other domain).

The algorithm for FIB aggregation is also a key factor that can affect the FIB size when content moves. *E.g.*, on a router R, 3 names (/n1, /n2, /n3) are going to one interface f_1, while the 4th (/n4) goes to a second interface f_2. Both FIBs shown in Table 3.1 can get the correct outgoing interface for each name, but the size of the FIBs is different. The aggregation gets even more complicated when there are multiple levels in the name tree and multiple outgoing interfaces for each name. For our calculation, we used a recursive program to try every possible outgoing interface combination (including no aggregation) at each level of the name tree to get the optimal result in all the situations. The process is accelerated by dynamic programming which stores the optimal result for the chosen aggregation earlier.

Since there are 2 basic ways of implementing the FIB (whether we treat multiple outgoing interface for the same name as one entry or multiple entries), we study 2 different metrics for this evaluation: the total number of names, and the sum of outgoing face counts for each name (referred to as the number of entries). The number of names and number of entries among all the FIBs in the topology as the

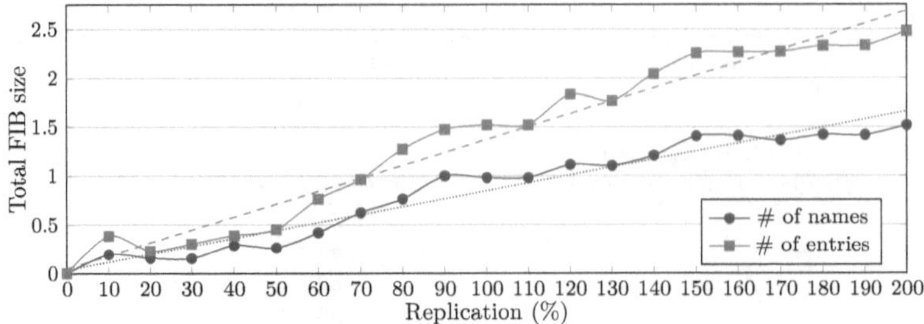

Figure 3.2: **Total FIB size (M)** *vs.* **data replication proportion.**

name replication percentage increases is shown in Figure 3.2. We see that when all the content follow the domain hierarchy (similar to IP), the aggregation performs well and the total FIB size in the network is only 2,078 ($\sim$20 entries per router on average). But the FIB size is affected significantly even when a small portion of data is replicated — the total number of entries reaches around 400,000 even when there is 10% replication. When the replication reaches 200%, the total number of names reaches 1.5×10^6 while the total number of entries reaches 2.5×10^6.

We can also see that the FIB size (either # of names or # of entries) grows linearly with the percentage of replication (marked as dashed and dotted lines in the figure). With content being replicated more in the network (which is a common trend and a desirable feature in ICN), the aggregate-ability of hierarchical names drops significantly. Note that we are using a relatively small data set compared to the amount of content available at Internet scale. With such a large number of content names, it is almost impossible to perform the algorithm to calculate "optimal" FIB size (off-line solution that tries all the combinations). For the online solution which adds entries when a content item is replicated, the number of names in the FIB can easily approach the number of total names, even with small replication percentage. In our evaluation, the average number of names in each FIB reaches 5.4×10^5 (54% of the name space) when each data is replicated once.

3.2.2 Discussion

To deal with the lack of aggregate-ability, SNAMP [127] has been proposed as a way to scale the forwarding in NDN. It divides the network into zones (similar to what we did here at the beginning of the evaluation) and use a distributed name mapping system NDNS (similar to DNS in IP and GNRS in MF) to store the mapping of content names to the zones that have the content. When the routers do not know how to forward an Interest packet, they first send a NACK to the consumer. The consumer then requests the NDNS for the name of zones containing the content, and attaches the response (a set of zones) in the Interest packet. The intermediate routers can then forward the Interest based on either the name or the zones (as hints).

With SNAMP, the routers only need to have FIB entries for the zones, which is much smaller than the name space size. However, there are still several issues with the solution: *1*) it creates higher burden on each router to lookup both the *content name* and the zone name(s); *2*) the end hosts will now have to perform an extra lookup for the content; *3*) the lookup on the end hosts is similar to a DNS lookup in IP which is essentially an early binding. Such a mechanism poses difficulties when dealing with content mobility; *4*) the scalability of NDNS itself can be difficult since it has to store each name and the zones serving the name.

Therefore, the benefit of aggregate-ability with hierarchical names cannot be fully exploited in an ICN, at least with existing solutions.

3.3 Comparison 3: semantics & manageability

Other than the aggregate-ability, hierarchical names also embeds the hierarchical semantics and the logic of hierarchical name space management in the network layer. In this section, we examine the benefits and the issues with this choice.

3.3.1 Hierarchical semantics

Placing the hierarchical semantics in the network layer can get benefit in some applications and use cases. *E.g.*, a data consumer can query ABC sports news using name `/ABC/sports`, he can also give a more detailed query, say `/ABC/sports/football/superbowl/2016`. In a publish/subscribe (pub/-sub) system [3], a publication containing name `/ABC/sports/football` can be disseminated to all the subscribers subscribing to `/ABC`, `/ABC/sports` and `/ABC/sports/football`. The hierarchical names can reduce the load in the network since one packet can be disseminated to multiple groups.

However, the applications will face dilemma when the relationship among the contents are not following the hierarchy. *E.g.*, in a building management system, a light L in room 302 can be named as: `/building/lights/floor3/room- 302/L` or `/building/floor3/lights/room302/L`, or `/building/floor3/room302/lights/L`.

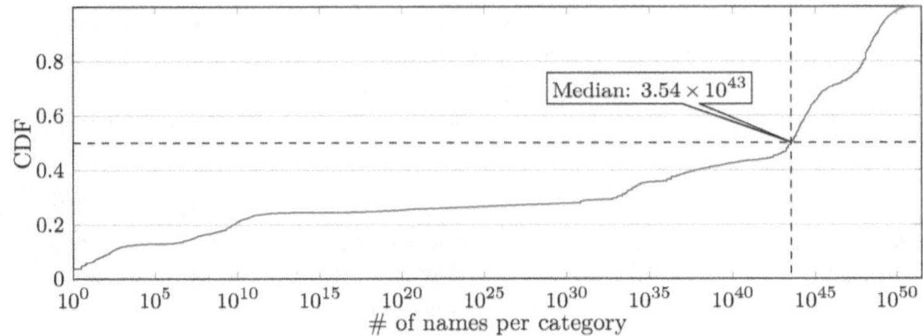

Figure 3.3: **Number of names per category in Wikipedia with hierarchical names.**

Similar situation is seen in the communication system among the first responders of emergency. Should a police station in area A use name `/areaA/police` or `/police/ areaA`? With the first naming schema, we can enable the commander to send messages to all the first responders in area A (using `/areaA` directly), while the second naming schema enables the top police department to send message to all the police departments in different areas (using `/police`). It is also quite common for ABC to publish a piece of news covering both sports and financial topics.

One might say that we can create different names for these content objects to optimize the reach-ability of them. However, this solution can cause the expansion of the name space and yield lower aggregate-ability and larger FIB size. To study the effect of the expansion, we took a representative of knowledge base, which is believed to follow a hierarchy, Wikipedia (a dump created on 2014.04.02) as our data set. Wikipedia has a category system which maintains the "IsA" relationship among different concepts. *E.g.*, page "NDN" belongs to category "Computer networking" which further belongs to 3 categories: "Telecommunications", "Computing", and "Data transmission". All these categories are rooted at a category called "Main topic classifications". To ensure the reach-ability of all the categories, we trace the category relationships from each category to main topic classifications. Each path (avoiding loops) will be translated into a name. *E.g.*, "NDN" can have names `/.../Telecommunications/Computer- networking/NDN`, `/.../Computing/Computernet- working/NDN`, and `/.../Datatransmission/Com- puternetworking/NDN` since people who are interested in telecommunications, computing, *etc.*, should also be able to reach the page of NDN.

The CDF of names per category is shown in Figure 3.3. Due to the complex relationship, the categories can have a lot of paths towards the top classification category. Although we only have 989,468 categories in the data set, the average names per category is 5.5×10^{48}, and the maximum even reaches 3.06×10^{51}. The size of the name space is expanded to 6.07×10^{54}, much larger than the 10^6 "flat" name space.

From the result, we can see that the name space would expand a lot while trying to convert a mesh-like name space to a hierarchical one. Similar examples can be found in any "tag-based" applications or data pools powered by search engines. With the advent of the tags, hyper-links, and powerful search engines, we can see that the semantics of the contents are no longer following strict hierarchies. The relationship among them can be more complex and form a directed graph. Therefore, we start to wonder, if it is still a good choice to place the hierarchical semantics in the network layer? Or should we leave them in the application layer so that different applications can have different choices of their own naming schema.

3.3.2 Hierarchical name space management

Another feature the hierarchical name provides is the hierarchical name space management. In this schema, each entity can have a name space and distribute a sub name space to an entity that belongs to it. *E.g.*, IEEE can have a name space `/IEEE` and give a sub name space to LANMAN (`/IEEE/LANMAN`) who can further distribute sub name spaces (`/IEEE/LANMAN/papers/...`) to each paper. With the hierarchical name space management, the network can also enforce policy on some prefixes, *e.g.*, give priority to content under `/emergency` will allow prioritization for the communication among emergency management authorities. However, this schema can also cause "suffix hole" [128] problem when using with LPM in forwarding. We assume that a person has a name space `/P`, and he gives a sub name space `/P/photos` to store his pictures. This person has a desktop at home and a laptop that he carries.The desktop serves most of his documents including *some of* the photos therefore it will propagate the prefix `/P`. But the laptop only serves *some of* his photos and therefore it will propagate prefix `/P/photos`. When there is a request to a photo, it will be forwarded to the laptop due to the LPM no matter if the photo is stored on the laptop or desktop. The problem affects the reach-ability of the contents since the desktop cannot get requests on photos even if it has the data.

To ensure the content reach-ability, the desktop in our example has to propagate both `/P` and `/P/photos` explicitly so that the LPM can return 2 sources on photos. But we argue that for a name space with many levels, and shared among multiple end hosts, it is very difficult to synchronize the name space propagation. Even if the applications find a way to synchronize the propagation, the solution would result in a lot more FIB entries being propagated in the network and affect the aggregate-ability of hierarchical names.

3.4 Chapter summary

In this chapter, we compared hierarchical *vs.* flat n aming s chema f or I CN across
several important metrics, some of which are interdependent. Our comparison
show that: *1*) The complexity of performing lookups of hierarchical names is much
higher due to the need to parse each component of the name and then lookup for
individual entries to determine the outgoing interface; *2*) With aggregate-ability,
hierarchical names reduce the FIB size. However, aggregate-ability is diminished
by content movement/replication, thus making the heavy-weight LPM forwarding
inefficient; *3*) Enforcing hierarchical name semantics might still not satisfy all the
applications. Content relationships with mesh-like structures (*e.g.*, Wikipedia) can
still cause name space explosion; *4*) The suffix hole problem caused by hierarchical
names results in more complicated name space management, resulting in more FIB
entries being propagated in the network;

We do appreciate the expressiveness of hierarchical semantics, better name space
management. These are all desired by applications and supporting them in the
network layer has the potential to reduce the network traffic and improve caching
efficiency. However, information structures are much more complex nowadays than
just strict hierarchies. Especially as reflected i n t he g raph b ased s tructures that
come from social networks, communities of interest and the relationships of data in
information bases such as Wikipedia. When these are represented by hierarchies, it
results in multiple different hierarchies to represent each possible relationship. As
a consequence the name space explodes very quickly, as reflected i n o ur a nalysis of
the name space for the Wikipedia dataset. However, a naming framework that is
agnostic to these relationships, potentially by uniquely identifying each independent
data item distinctly, results in a much more limited growth in the name space. A flat
naming framework is agnostic to the structure of the data. Since most approaches
for accessing information over the network involve a mapping from a user requested
name to a name appropriate to the network, a flat n aming framework is likely to be
much more scalable at the network layer, even though clearly at the user and data
organization involves relationships and hierarchies.

Chapter 4

ISI: Integrate Sensor Networks to Internet with ICN

IoT is a growing topic of interest and Billions of IoT devices are expected to connect to the Internet in the near future. IoT devices generally operate with constrained resources and hence, they differ from the traditional devices operated in the Internet. In this chapter, we show that ICN, a new networking paradigm, is a more suitable architecture for the IoT environment compared to the currently prevailing IP based network. We observe that recent works which propose to use ICN for IoT, either do not cover the need to integrate *Sensor Networks* with the Internet to realize IoT or do so inefficiently. There is a need to understand effective ways to integrate the various heterogeneous *Sensor Networks* with the Internet without affecting their current mode of operation. Therefore, this chapter studies the essential requirements for integrating *Sensor Networks* to the Internet. Essentially, this chapter provides an architecture with *Gateways* for paving a way for the *Sensor Networks* to become a part of the IoT family. We further provide a naming schema for efficient operation of the resource constrained *Sensor Networks*, and discuss mobility, security, communication patterns and propose the most suitable choices for efficient operation of the IoT networks with ICN.

The key contributions in this work include:

- Analysis of the requirements for an architecture to integrate *Sensor Networks* with the Internet.
- Architecture *ISI*: to integrate *Sensor Networks* to the Internet with ICN.
- Naming schema for the IoT networks operating with ICN.
- Communication protocol for the IoT networks.
- Discussion on the aspect of Mobility and Security for IoT.

Contents

4.1 Use case formalization

In this section, we formalize some essential use cases that will help derive the requirements for integrating *Sensor Networks* to the Internet. These requirements form the basis for building the proposed *ISI* architecture.

We take the example of a smart city as shown in Figure.4.1 with many buildings equipped with *Sensor Networks* to build our use cases. Let us consider an application that monitors the temperature of all the rooms in a smart building as a representative *Sensor Network*. The smart building has several rooms equipped with temperature sensitive machinery *e.g.*, servers and hence each room is equipped with a temperature sensing sensor device. There is a Base Station (BS) that gathers the temperature from each room every 30mins and raises an alarm when abnormalities occur. Several such scenarios can be gathered in a smart city *e.g.*, in Industrial units, offices, smart

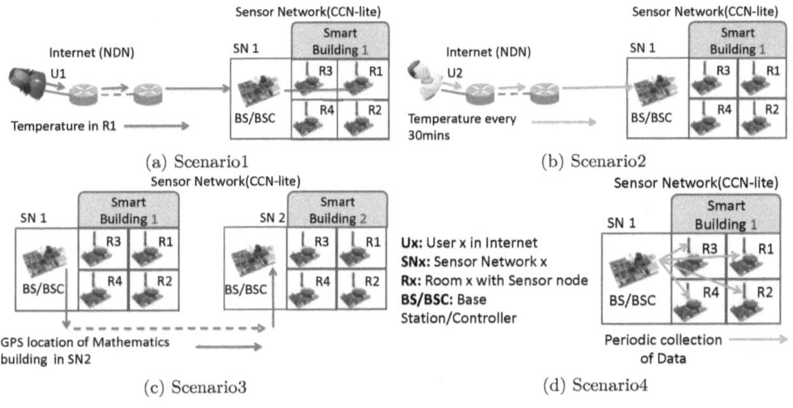

Figure 4.1: **Use cases scenarios.**

houses for controlling fire, *etc.* Let us consider that, *Sensor Network 1* (SN1) is operating in the building 1 which is a Computer Science building in a university, and *Sensor Network 2* (SN2) is operating in the building 2 which is a Mathematics building in the same university.

Scenario 1: A user (U1) (*e.g.*, a system administrator) in the Internet is interested in the temperature of room 1 in the building 1. U1 is using the Internet operating with an ICN protocol like NDN [1]. However the building 1 is located in SN1 that runs a lighter version of an ICN protocol like CCN-lite [20]. Besides, U1 is interested in the temperature of room1 sensed by the sensor device S1 which is not awake all the time in order to save its constrained resources like power. U1 is not aware of the time at which S1 will be available to serve the requested content, nor the exact protocol used in the SN1.

Scenario 2: A user (U2) in the Internet is interested in receiving the cumulative temperature of the building 1 every 30mins. Similar to scenario 1, U2 is in the Internet but would like to receive the content collected and computed by the BS located in the *Sensor Network*.

Scenario 3: The Base Station 1 (BS1) in SN1 needs some content *e.g.*, the GPS location of the Mathematics building in the smart city. The mathematics building is located in SN2 of the smart city. The SN2 might be running the same or a different ICN protocol from SN1. BS1 is unaware of the location of the content or the protocol used in the SN2.

Scenario 4: Let us consider the operation of SN1. The sensor devices sense the temperature in each room periodically every 30mins. The BS1 is interested in the content produced by these sensing devices. The BS1 will gather the content and compute the cumulative temperature of the entire building and will raise an alarm when it observes abnormalities. BS1 wants to collect this information efficiently so as to ensure the maximum utilization of available resources in the constrained sensing devices in the SN1.

With the help of the above mentioned use cases we show the need for a protocol translation between the heterogeneous networks: Internet and *Sensor Network*, including communication between *Sensor Networks* operating different protocols. We also identify the lack of information regarding the nature of the *Sensor Network* for the users in the Internet, the different types of content requested by the users from Internet and different types of *Sensor Networks* and the vital issue of efficient utilization of the constrained resources to gather information within a *Sensor Network*. Although we use these four use cases here to derive the requirements for *ISI*, we can derive many more requirements and even different requirements based on the nature of the *Sensor Network* used as a representative. However, these basic use cases can be applied/extended to all *Sensor Networks* and *ISI* can easily support additional use cases.

4.2 Requirement analysis

In this section we build on our use cases to derive the various requirements for integrating the *Sensor Networks* with the Internet. We assume that *Sensor Networks* are operating with a lighter version of the ICN protocol like CCN-lite [20] (or NDN-lite) while the Internet operates with the full ICN stack like complete CCN/NDN [6] stack. We choose these architectures as representative for ICN, similar requirements will apply to other ICN architectures like MF [2], *etc.*

Gateway: We observe from use case 1, 2 and 3 that there are multitude of users scattered across hybrid *Sensor Networks* and Internet. However these networks don't use the same protocol. There is a need for protocol translation among these networks for communicating with each other. An efficient way to interface networks operating different protocols is via a *Gateway*. The *Gateway* should run the protocols of all the networks that it serves. The *Gateway* should be equipped with necessary intelligence and data structures to perform near transparent flow of traffic between the two networks to seamlessly integrate the networks.

Naming: ICN is a name based protocol and supports, unbounded and any length namespace. We observe from all the four use cases a need for a naming schema that is catered towards the operation of the constrained devices in the *Sensor Networks*. The rationale for this requirement is the MTU in the *Sensor Networks* is much smaller (127B) when compared to the MTU (1280B) used by the devices in the Internet. Hence, there is a need for smaller ICN names that can not only fit into the MTU of the *Sensor Networks* devices but also requires less storage on the forwarding engines of the sensing devices. Such a naming schema will ensure that IoT networks resources are used efficiently and will further ease their scalability.

Communication Protocol: All the four use cases present a different form of communication model: query/response (1&3) or pub/sub (2&4). In many *Sensor Networks*, there is usually a Base Station (BS) that collects the data sensed by the sensors in the network. Another common pattern is when a Base Station Controller (BSC) controls the sensor devices/actuators by sending control messages to them. We can notice that, unlike IP, the users in these networks are interested in the content similar to ICN irrespective of their location. With an efficient communication protocol we can ensure efficient utilization of the constrained resources in the *Sensor Networks*. *E.g.*, in use case 2&4, the user U2 and BS can use pub/sub to collect the data periodically. Additionally, with ICN in Internet we can benefit with the caching as it not only reduces the traffic in the core network, but will also reduce the traffic entering the resource constrained IoT networks. This ensures maximum availability of the content even when the sensing devices are sleeping to save resources.

Mobility: In addition to the usecases mentioned in Section 4.1, another and a more important aspect to consider is the mobility of sensor devices. The IoT networks should also be able to handle the mobility of sensor devices from one domain to another. Mobility may affect the naming, reachability and many other aspects of the moving devices.

Security: Security is a greater concern in many if not all of the *Sensor Networks* and the Internet. There is a growing concern that IoT's are designed without addressing many of the associated security concerns [129]. However, security induces additional overhead especially in the *Sensor Networks*. Hence, there is a need to analyze and provide security measures that meet the security requirement of the *Sensor Networks* and will not be an overkill with regards to their constrained resources.

4.3 Architecture

In this section we describe the proposed *ISI* architecture shown in Figure. 4.2 for integrating the various hybrid *Sensor Networks* to the Internet.

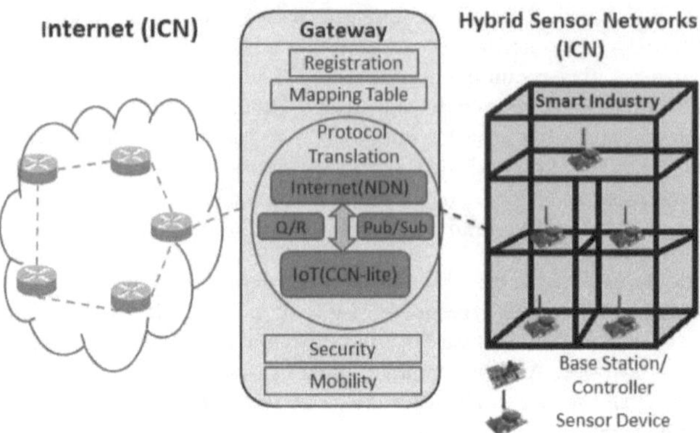

Figure 4.2: **The *ISI* architecture.**

4.3.1 Components

NDN network: We choose NDN as a representative ICN architecture. In principal it could be any ICN architecture. The underlying network is capable of retrieving *Content* from publishers in both the Internet as well as the IoT network. The network is also capable of delivering control messages to the *Sensor Networks*.

Sensor Networks: There are many hybrid *Sensor Networks* that represent numerous applications. Further, the *Sensor Networks* usually contain hybrid devices. The devices can have wireless or wired access. They can operate for the purpose of monitoring, controlling, *etc.* As discussed earlier, in this chapter, we propose that *Sensor Networks* should operate with the ICN protocols. Hence, we use a lighter version of the CCN called CCN-lite [20] for communication in the *Sensor Networks*. The *Sensor Networks* usually contain a BS or a BSC that collects the data sensed by the devices in the network for monitoring purpose or to control their operation. The *BS/BSC* are usually powerful machines and not constrained in resources unlike the sensing devices.

Gateway: This is the most essential piece of the proposed design. The *Gateway* sits between the Internet operating with the NDN protocol and the *Sensor Networks* operating with the CCN-lite protocol. All the traffic to/from the Internet and *Sensor Networks* has to pass through the *Gateway*. The main function of *Gateway* is to perform protocol translation between the two networks. The *Gateway* is also responsible for mapping functions (discussed shortly). It is clear that since the

IPv6 MTU is 1280B while the IEEE 802.15.4 can support only 127B, the authors in the IETF standard [18] suggest that header compression in IPv6 is unavoidable. However, the content generated in the *Sensor Network* is assumed to be small. We believe that with efficient designs of ICN names in the *Sensor Network* the *Gateway* does not have to compress the headers. Although we speak about one *Gateway* between the Internet and each *Sensor Network*, there is no restriction on the number of *Gateways*. As the traffic exchange between the Internet and *Sensor Networks* increases, the burden on a single *Gateway* also increases. Hence, multiple *Gateways* should be used to distribute the load.

4.3.2 Description

As said earlier, we assume that Internet is operating with the NDN protocol. While various *Sensor Networks* that represent applications like environmental monitoring, smart houses, *etc.*, are operating with the CCN-lite protocol. The users are spread across both the Internet as well as the *Sensor Networks*. The aim of this design is to let the applications operate in the *Sensor Networks* as they desire but extend their availability and control by integrating them with the Internet. The design allows the users in the Internet to access/control the IoT devices using the Internet. A key to achieve this integration is through *Gateways*.

The *Gateway* is a powerful component that has many roles to play. Every *Sensor Network* is associated with one or more *Gateways* that is responsible for seamlessly integrating the respective *Sensor Network* with the Internet. The entire traffic between these two worlds will flow through the *Gateway* transparent to the users in both the networks.

The *Gateway* runs both the NDN protocol and the CCN-lite protocol. The *Gateway* maintains a mapping table which maps the lengthy, unbounded names form the Internet running the NDN protocol to their equivalent short names in the *Sensor Networks* running the CCN-lite protocol.

The *Gateway* provides a registration procedure for every device in the *Sensor Network*. Each device upon entering the network must register itself with the *Gateway*. The *Gateway* provides an ID to each newly added device. The device then registers the short name and long name of the Content that it wishes to serve. These entries will be added to the mapping table maintained in the *Gateway*. The mapping table should be updated whenever there are any changes in the content served by the *Sensor Network*.

We will use the term *Inbound traffic* for the traffic entering the *Sensor Network* and the term *Outbound traffic* for the traffic going out of the *Sensor Network*. The inbound traffic from the users can be either a request for data or a request containing a control message. There are two possible outbound traffics: *1)* the reply to the inbound traffic and, *2)* the request/subscription traffic generated inside the *Sensor Network*. The two types of outbound traffics should be distinguished form one another as the reply traffic needs a name change through a mapping table lookup. This can be achieved by using any one bit available field in the packets.

When the *Gateway* receives inbound traffic it is basically a NDN Interest packet. The *Gateway* scans the mapping table to find the equivalent short name. The *Gateway* creates a CCN-lite Interest packet with the short name and forwards it to the *Sensor Network*. Upon receiving a CCN-lite Data packet from the *Sensor Network*, the *Gateway* performs a lookup in the mapping table to find the long name and creates a NDN Data packet with the long name, extracts the Content from the CCN-lite Data packet and inserts it into the NDN Data packet and forwards it in the Internet.

Another type of out bound traffic is basically a CCN-lite Interest for content located either in the Internet or in other IoT network. The *Gateways* also support inter IoT network communication. When an IoT network running a certain application needs information from outside its network, it simply generates a CCN-lite Interest and forwards it to the *Gateway*. Since this is an outbound request traffic the *Gateway* simply translates it to a NDN Interest and forwards it in the network. It eventually reaches the intended publisher in the Internet or the *Gateway* associated with the target *Sensor Network*. When the publisher is located in Internet, it follows the standard NDN protocol and reply with the corresponding data packet. If the Interest reaches a *Gateway* associated to another *Sensor Network*, the *Gateway* performs a mapping table lookup to fetch the equivalent short name and prepares a CCN-lite Interest and forwards it to the *Sensor Network*. Upon receiving the Data packet it prepares the NDN Data packet as explained earlier and forwards it to the Internet. The data packet eventually reaches the *Gateway* of the *Sensor Network* that initiated the request. The *Gateway* performs a mere protocol translation and generates the CCN-lite Data packet as described earlier and forwards it to user in the *Sensor Network*.

4.4 Naming schema for *Sensor Networks*

4.4.1 Naming in IoT

The IoT devices are usually equipped with the Ethernet technology like IEEE 802.15.4 and Bluetooth LE. This results in a much smaller MTU (127B) compared to the traditional layer-2 technologies adopted in the Internet. This raises a concern on the size of the packets that traverse the IoT network. One way to reduce the packet size is to have smaller names that are relevant to the IoT networks. The any length, unbounded hierarchically structured names defined by many ICN architectures do not suit the IoT networks. The naming schema for IoT should create precise names to serve the purpose of the application and yet be specific and small.

We describe our naming schema using the same example of the smart city with *Sensor Networks* as shown in Figure. 4.2. Let us consider the same application of monitoring the temperature of all the rooms in a smart building from our use cases in §4.1. We know that each room in the smart building is equipped with temperature sensing sensor devices and BS collects the data generated by the sensing devices.

We propose a naming structure of the form *Metric/ID/Area/Date/Time*. The first component *Metric* specifies what kind of data is generated by the sensing device *e.g.*, temperature, pressure, humidity, *etc.* The second component *ID* represents the unique identifier assigned to the device in the *Sensor Network*. The third component *Area* specifies the location/geographic range covered by the sensing device *e.g.*, room, building, GPS location, *etc.* The fourth component *Date* specifies the day at which the readings are measured and the fifth component *Time* specifies the time at which the reading was captured by the device. The granularity of each component can be application dependant *e.g.*, the time can vary from hours to seconds to minutes or more. Applying this naming schema to our smart building example the temperature sensed by a device with the id 01 in the room1 on 3rd November 2016 at 12:30 could be retrieved with a name */temp/01/r1/03-11-16/12:30*. This name is only 26B, leaving the rest of the packet for the content.

In most *Sensor Networks* the BS usually collects the data periodically from the sensing devices in the network. To distinguish the data retrieved from the BS we can use a naming schema of the form */Metric/BS/Area/Date/Time*. Note that the component *Area* in the naming schema for IoT represents individual rooms whereas it represent the whole building in case of the BS. Thus, a user in NDN network can request for temperature of the whole building or for the individual rooms. This naming schema is fairly general and similar names can be created for different IoT networks based on specifics of the area or application of the IoT devices used in the network.

4.4.2 Naming in the Internet

Recent ICN proposals such as NDN [6] and COPSS [3] adopt human-readable, hierarchically structured Names and Content Descriptors (CDs). Continuing our smart building example, a possible name structure for renaming the content for the Internet could be */temperature/UNI/ComputerScience/Building1/03-11-16/12:30* for the temperature of the Computer Science building in the university on 3rd November 2016 at 12:30 and */temperature/UNI/ComputerScience/Building1/room1/03-11-16/12:30* for the temperature of room1 at 12:30. We allow the availability of data sensed in every room in the Internet as some rooms might be sensitive to temperature and would have to be monitored *e.g.*, the temperature of a server room.

4.5 Communication protocol for IoT and Internet

In this section we discuss the current communication protocols and propose the suitable communication protocol for IoT and ICN based Internet.

4.5.1 Query/Response (Q/R) communication

This is a dominant mode of communication in current networks (both IP and ICN). A user interested in some content simply queries the network with the request for data. Any producer of the content (or also a node with an available copy of the data in case of ICN) responds to the request with the data.

4.5.1.1 Q/R communication in IoT

In *Sensor Networks* the BS can query the sensing devices to retrieve the sensed data. The BS simply generates a request with the respective *content name* and forwards it to the network. Upon reaching the producer, the sensing device responds with the requested content. The BS can also send control messages using the query/response mode where the query can contain the control command while the response can contain an acknowledgement of the action taken. The IoT devices can also query for content located in the Internet or other IoT networks. The *Gateway* should assist in retrieving the content in this case.

4.5.1.2 Q/R communication in the Internet

A user in the Internet generates an ICN request (Interest) with the *content name* of the desired content and forwards it in the network. If the content is located in the caches of any intermediate forwarding node then the cached copy is returned to the user. Otherwise the Interest eventually reaches the producer who replies with the requested content. If the producer is located in an IoT network, then the *Gateway* will assist in retrieving the content however, this will be transparent to the user.

4.5.2 Publish/Subscribe (pub/sub) communication

In a pub/sub scenario, there are essentially two roles: publisher and subscriber. The publishers usually generate some data that could be of interest to subscribers. The subscribers maintain a long term subscriptions to the content published by the publishers (refer to COPSS [3] for detail). Whenever a piece of content is published by the publishers, the network will deliver it to all of its subscribers.

4.5.2.1 Pub/sub communication in IoT

In IoT, the sensing devices that periodically sense the data can take up the role of publisher and publish the sensed data periodically. The BS is the subscriber interested in these contents and hence it will subscribe to these contents and will receive them as and when they are published.

4.5.2.2 Pub/sub communication in the Internet

Similar to IoT, publishers and subscribers exist in the ICN based Internet too. The users in the Internet can not only subscribe to the content published inside the Internet but also to the content published in the IoT networks.

4.5.3 Communication protocol for IoT

There are two possible types of communication that can take place in the IoT networks: *1)* within the *Sensor Networks*. *2)* with Internet/other Sensor Networks. The nature of communication in these networks is different and can greatly affect the design choices of an efficient communication protocol for the *Sensor Networks*.

In *Sensor Networks*, the devices usually sense the respective data periodically while the BS gathers the sensed data and analyzes it to take necessary actions. Therefore, the pub/sub communication model seems more suitable in this scenario. The devices can behave like publishers and publish the data periodically. While the

BS can behave like the subscriber that subscribes to the data published by all the devices in its *Sensor Network*. This design choice allows the resource constrained sensor devices to efficiently utilize their battery power by waking up only to sense and publish the data. We agree, that there are chances for the packets to get lost. Hence, for reliability reason we propose the BS to resume to Q/R to retrieve only the data that was lost during the next periodic cycle when the sensing device is awake to sense the next reading. However, during Q/R we expect the sensor device to wait for an acknowledgement before going back to sleep to ensure that BS has received the packet this time. This also means that a sensing device should retain some of its previously sensed data, which we believe can be configured based on the applications requirement *e.g.*, three most recent readings for reliability.

In the Internet, Q/R is the dominant form of communication (both in IP and ICN). However, for communicating with the Sensor Networks we can choose between Q/R and Pub/Sub based on the needs of the user. If a user (or any other application or *Sensor Network*) is interested in periodically receiving the data collected by the *Sensor Networks*, then Pub/Sub is the ideal choice for communication. To reduce the burden on resource constrained sensing devices in the *Sensor Network*, we believe that caching can be enabled on the BS. Other sensing devices can choose to retain or turn off caching based on their available resources. Since the BS gathers the data from all the sensors, it can act as a publisher to the subscribers in the Internet. Please note that the subscribers in the Internet will subscribe to the longer names and not the shorter names used for publishing inside the *Sensor Networks*. Hence, the *Gateway* has to create new publication data packets with their equivalent long names from the mapping table and then forward it to the users in the Internet. Another and most likely a common scenario is when users in the Internet are interested in some particular data generated in the *Sensor Networks* or if they would like to send some control message to the *Sensor Networks*. Intuitively, Q/R seems ideal for such scenarios. When a user is interested in some data he/she can generate a CCN *Interest* with the longer *content name* and the network will forward the packet to the *Gateway*. Once the *Gateway* receives the packet it performs a protocol translation from CCN to CCN-lite and generates a CCN-lite *Interest* with the equivalent short name from the mapping table and forwards it to the BS/BSC. Based on the type of the request received the BS/BSC either replies with the requested data or an acknowledgement for the action taken by the BS/BSC.

4.6 Use case realization

This section describes the *ISI* architecture by leveraging the use cases from §4.1.

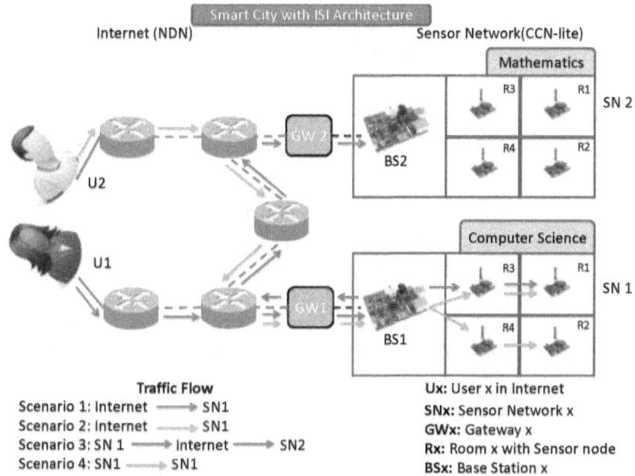

Figure 4.3: **Smart city use cases with ISI architecture.**

Consider the example network topology of a smart city with *ISI* architecture as shown in Figure. 4.3. There is a BS in each *Sensor Network* that collects the temperature sensed by the devices periodically every 30mins. Each network is attached to a *Gateway* that runs both the NDN and CCN-lite protocols for interconnecting the *Sensor Networks* and the Internet.

Scenario 1: A user (U1) in the Internet is interested in the temperature of room1 in the building1. So, U1 will generate a NDN Interest with the name */temperature/UNI/ComputerScience/Building1/room1/03-11-16/12:30*. The network will forward the Interest to *Gateway*1 (GW1). GW1 will check its mapping table for the name. When no match is found, the GW1 behaves like a router and the NDN module running inside the GW1 will handle this packet by forwarding it to the appropriate router in the Internet. If there is a match, the GW1 will generate a CCN-lite Interest with the equivalent short name */temp/01/r1/03-11-16/12:30* and forward it to the CCN-lite module which in turn will forward it to the BS1. Since the BS1 periodically collects all the data, it will generate the CCN-lite data with the requested content and forward it to GW1; otherwise it is forwarded to the device S1 in the *Sensor Network1*. Upon receiving a CCN-lite data, the *Gateway* will scan its mapping table to find the respective short name. If there is a match the GW1 will extract the content from the CCN-lite data packet, generate a CCN data packet with the equivalent long name with the extracted content and forward it in the Internet. When there is no match found in the mapping table the GW1 will discard the data packet.

Scenario 2: A user (U2) in the Internet is interested in receiving the temperature of the Computer Science building every 30mins. U2 will subscribe to the Content Descriptor (CD) */temperature/UNI/ComputerScience/Building1/*. Every 30mins, when BS1 has received the temperature of each room in the building, it will calculate the temperature of the building and publish a CCN-lite data with the name */temp/BS/Building1/Date/Time* (the parameter Date and Time should be replaced with the respective values). When the GW1 receives this packet it will check its mapping table and generate a CCN publication packet with the equivalent long name and the content and forward it to the subscribers in the Internet.

Scenario 3: The BS1 in the SN1 needs some content say the GPS location of the Mathematics building in the smart city. It generates a CCN-lite Interest with the *content name /GPS/Location/UNI/Mathematics/Building2/* and forwards it to GW1. Please note that since this is an outbound traffic for content located outside the *Sensor Network* this should be indicated by setting any available bit in the Interest packet. For CCN-lite the EXCLUDE field can be used to indicate this. Upon receiving this Interest, the GW1 identifies it as an outbound traffic by inspecting the one bit field. The *Gateway* will only perform a protocol translation by generating a CCN Interest with the same name and forward it to the Internet. The content may be located in the Internet or also in another *Sensor Network*. The publisher either from the Internet or any other *Sensor Network* (with the help of its *Gateway* similar to scenario1) will reply with the content. Upon receiving a data packet the GW1 will again perform a protocol translation by extracting the content from the CCN data packet and generate the CCN-lite data packet with the content and forward it to BS1.

Scenario 4: Scenario4 consideres the internal operation of *Sensor Network1*. The sensor devices are sensing the temperature of the room every 30mins. They are the publishers and will publish a packet every 30mins with the name */temp/id/-room_no/Date/Time, e.g., /temp/01/r1/03-11-16/12:30*. The BS1 has subscribed to the prefix */temp* and hence will receive the data sensed by all the sensors as and when it is published.

There are chances for the packets to get lost. If there is any packet loss, then the BS1 will generate a CCN-lite Interest with the specific name. *E.g.*, if the packet from the S2 was lost then the BS1 will send a CCN-lite Interest with the name */temp/02/r2/03-11-16/12:30* at the next 30mins cycle when the S2 will wake up to sense the next temperature reading. For reliability reasons we require the sensors to store their latest three readings. When S2 receives an Interest, it will reply with the requested content. We suggest the device S2 to stay awake for at least 1RTT for the acknowledgement from BS1 to ensure that BS1 has received the data this time.

4.7 Discussions

4.7.1 Mobility

Nowadays mobility has become a norm and IoT devices will bear no exception to fulfill this requirement, especially with emerging new-generation applications like smart-city, smart-home, *etc.* A simple example is when a smart car in a smart city moves from building 1 to building2. During this mobility, the smart car is detaching from the *Sensor Network* in building1 and is attaching to *Sensor Network* in building 2.

In order to support mobility, the *Gateway* must handle the devices that move from one domain to another. The *Gateway* can either offer a Time To Live (TTL) during registration and/or offer a de-registration process. During de-registration, the smart car sends an Interest with the de-registration request to *Gateway* and the *Gateway* responds with an acknowledgement. The car can choose to wait for the acknowledgement or not. When the car moves to another domain it again registers itself with the associated *Gateway* of the new domain. Even if the de-registration packet was lost, since the car has registered to anther *Gateway* the network will synchronize with the routing updates.

4.7.2 Security

4.7.2.1 Security in IoT

IEEE 802.15.4 provides the capability for some link-layer security. The authors in IETF standard [18] urge users to make use of it. A majority of the sensor devices in *Sensor Networks* are expected to operate within their networks. Acknowledging resource constraints in the IoT devices, we believe they should be equipped with the minimum level of security features necessary for their operation. The asymmetric key encryption is computationally complex for the *Sensor Networks* [80], so we suggest the devices in the *Sensor Networks* can use the features provided at the link layer for encryption and if additional security is desired then opt for symmetric key encryption.

Moreover, the *Sensor Networks* will benefit with the content based security provided by the ICN solutions. Interestingly, authors in [130] discuss Attribute Based Encryption (ABE) for ICN networks. However, the current ABE solution are heavy

for the IoT networks. The Internet on the other hand can benefit greatly with ABE
while the Gateway can assist in encryption and decryption of the content using
light-weight security measures suitable for the IoT networks.

4.7.2.2 Security in the Internet

The devices in the Internet are subject to more attacks compared to devices in
the *Sensor Networks*. Moreover, the devices in the Internet are relatively powerful
compared to the devices in *Sensor Networks*. These devices are capable of handling
complex computation and hence can opt for asymmetric key encryption. Although it
is computational heavy, it is harder to decipher the content. ICN solutions inherently
provide security by securing the content unlike securing the communication link as
in IP. *E.g.*, NDN uses the digital signature of the publisher for authenticating all
the content and also uses encryption for protecting private content.

4.8 Chapter summary

In this chapter, we discussed the shortcomings of current IoT designs with a proposal
for leveraging ICN for realizing IoT; we observed that ICN is more suitable for
supporting the requirements of IoT compared to IP. We discussed in detail the
importance and requirements for incorporating *Sensor Networks* into the Internet,
thus paving a way for them to join the IoT family. We also observed that IoT
devices do not need the full NDN stack and can work with lighter versions like
CCN-lite/NDN-lite. We analyzed the various requirements for an architecture to
integrate the *Sensor Networks* to the Internet and proposed *ISI* architecture with
Gateways. We described in detail the responsibilities of such a *Gateway* and further
proposed a naming schema and communication protocol along with some possible
mobility and security considerations for the IoT networks. With the help of several
use cases we described the functionality of *ISI* architecture for realizing IoT with
ICN.

Chapter 5

Application - FOGG: A Fog Computing Based Gateway to Integrate Sensor Networks to Internet

Fog computing is a promising technology that brings computing closer to the end-users of the network. It offers numerous benefits especially, for IoT networks and hence, needs further investigation. Therefore, in this chapter, we employ the *ISI* architecture from Chapter 4 with Fog computing to propose an application named *FOGG: A Fog Computing Based Gateway to Integrate Sensor Networks to Internet*. *FOGG* uses the benefits of Fog computing with a dedicated device to function as an IoT gateway to provide the needed integration. In addition, *FOGG* also provides essential services like name/protocol translation, security and controller functionalities for IoT, close to the end-users.

Contents

5.1 Fog computing

Traditional Cloud based applications and services direct users requests to the nearby data centers for storage and computing. However, with increasing number of users and focus towards low-latency and high bandwidth requirements from applications like high definition video streaming, technologies like Fog computing [13] have emerged. Fog computing is a promising new architecture that utilizes the multitude of end-user/edge-devices to carry out various operations like, storing, computing, controlling, *etc.* Fog computing can improve the QoS experienced by users through deploying the required storage at the edge of the network *i.e.*, close to the end-users. Many applications like smart grids, sensor networks and industrial automation have already been realized with Fog computing. In PHOENIX, we argue that deployment of the future architectures like ICN can also greatly benefit with Fog computing as it expedites the process of integration with the existing technologies and exploits the heterogeneity of the devices available at the edge.

As discussed in Chapter 1&2, even though many recent works like [46, 47], *etc.*, focus on addressing different problems of IoT, they do not highlight the need to integrate the *Sensor Networks* with the Internet to realize IoT. Hence, in Chapter 4, we provided the *ISI* architecture to fulfill this vital need. The main goal of this chapter is to employ the *ISI* architecture to exploit the benefits provided by Fog computing. Accordingly, we propose *FOGG: A Fog Computing Based Gateway to Integrate Sensor Networks to Internet.* The primary focus of *FOGG* is to bridge the Internet (running on IP, ICN or other future protocols) with the IoT domains operating with ICN protocols. In the remainder of this chapter, we derive the various requirements for realizing such a Fog based – IoT = Internet + SN design and introduce *FOGG* which provides *Fog Gateways* to integrate the *Sensor Networks* with the Internet. To this end, *FOGG* is designed to provide Fog based services such

as name/protocol translation, security (secure onboarding), controller functionality
and *etc.* However, in this preliminary work, we mainly focus on the Fog based
name/protocol translation service.

5.2 Use cases and requirements

In this section, similar to Chapter 4, we formalize the essential use cases and derive
the requirements for integrating *Sensor Networks* to the Internet with Fog computing. These requirements will further assist in building *FOGG*.

5.2.1 Use case formalization

We consider the example of a smart industry with many divisions equipped with *Sensor Networks* to build our use cases. Let us consider the various applications that an
industry can house *e.g.*, monitoring the temperature of equipments like boilers, tak-
ing readings, sensor based actuators, *etc.*, as representative *Sensor Networks*. The
smart industry has several equipments, wherein each equipment is equipped with a
specific sensor device. There is a Base Station Controller (BSC) that gathers the
inputs like temperature readings and gives instructions for operating the actuators
from each room every 30mins. The BSC raises an alarm or notifies the administrator when abnormalities occur. Further, the *Sensor Network1* (SN1) constitutes the
sensor devices operating in the division1 and *Sensor Network2* (SN2) constitutes
the sensor devices operating in the division2 of the industrial unit.

Scenarios: We can consider three important use case scenarios in the above
mentioned smart industry example. In the first scenario, A user in the Internet is
interested in the temperature of equipment1 in division1. In the second scenario,
a sensor equipment E3 in SN1 needs some content *e.g.*, the accurate viscosity of
the liquid it boils from the equipment E3 in division2 in SN2. Finally, in the third
scenario, all the sensor devices need to transfer their readings periodically to the
Cloud for storage and further processing.

5.2.2 Requirement analysis

We assume that *Sensor Networks* operate with a lighter version of the ICN protocol
like the CCN-lite (or NDN-lite) [20] while the Internet can operate with IP and/or

ICN protocols like NDN. We choose NDN as a representative for ICN, similar requirements will apply to other future architectures like MF [2], XIA [7], *etc.* In addition to the requirements for a Gateway, Naming, Communication Protocol and Security in Chapter 4 (§4.2), in this chapter, we identify the necessary requirements for a controller in *FOGG*.

Controller: The *Sensor Networks* generate a lot of raw data that needs further processing. However, the sensor devices are heavily constrained in resources and cannot perform such operations. Additionally, transferring this raw data for computation and storage in Cloud is necessary but time consuming. This can prove to be expensive for the sensor devices as the Cloud might be operating with another protocol. Further, for latency sensitive applications such as in the industry, if the computation has to be carried out in the Cloud to raise an alarm for a fire it might lead to heavy damages and even risk lives. Additionally, the increasing amount of data generated by the Billions of hybrid IoT devices is already a concern in the Big Data community [131] along with the increasing amount of mobile data traffic [132]. However, most of the data generated by these devices is redundant and hence can be eliminated with some pre-processing before storing in the Cloud. There is a need for a dedicated controlling node equipped with the necessary intelligence, processing capability and associated data structures that can handle complex operations on behalf of the resource-constrained *Sensor Networks*. The controller node should also perform a near transparent flow of traffic between the *Sensor Networks* and Cloud.

5.3 *FOGG* design

In this section we describe the design of *FOGG* shown in Figure. 5.1 for integrating the various hybrid *Sensor Networks* with the Internet using Fog computing.

We assume that, Internet could be operating on IP or future protocols such as ICN while the different *Sensor Networks* that represent various applications like environmental monitoring, smart houses, *etc.*, could run on lighter versions of IP, ICN or other protocols. The users are spread across both the Internet as well as the *Sensor Networks*. The aim of *FOGG* is to let the devices operate in the *Sensor Networks* as they desire but extend their availability and control by integrating them with the Internet by introducing a *Fog Gateway* in the *Sensor Networks* that provides the necessary intelligence and processing capability. The design allows the users in the Internet to access/control the IoT devices using the Internet. A key to achieve this integration is through *Fog Gateways* at the edge of the *Sensor Networks*. Below, we provide details on how *FOGG* could leverage the computing provided by Fog nodes to better support the integration of various heterogeneous *Sensor Networks* with the Internet.

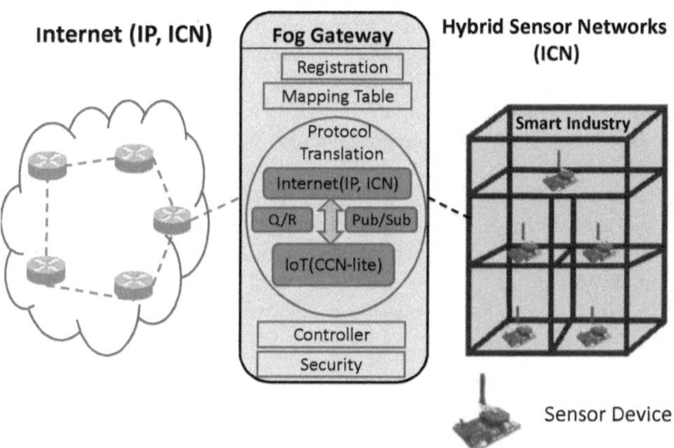

Figure 5.1: The *FOGG* design.

5.3.1 Controller functionality

In *FOGG*, we envision a powerful node that provides the functionalities of a Gateway (similar to the gateway in Chapter 4). We call this node the *Fog Gateway*. In addition to the functionalities of the gateway discussed in Chapter 4, the *Fog Gateway* is also capable of performing the tasks similar to that of a controller. *FOGG* can collect the data periodically from the sensor devices in the *Sensor Network* and can respond to the queries from Internet and other *Sensor Networks*. Similarly, *Fog Gateway* can also receive control messages from other networks and authorize and carry out the execution of controlling the devices in the *Sensor Network*.

5.3.2 Protocol translation

The *Fog Gateway* is a powerful component and provides various functionalities. Every *Sensor Network* is associated with one (or more) *Fog Gateway* that sit at the edge of the *Sensor Network*. This gateway is responsible for seamlessly integrating the respective *Sensor Network* with the Internet. The entire traffic between these two worlds will flow through the *Fog Gateway* transparent to the users in both the networks. The *Fog Gateway* runs the protocols used by both the Internet and the *Sensor Networks* in order to optimally translate between the two and in some cases behave transparent to the communication.

The *Fog Gateway* maintains a mapping table to map the source/destination addresses or content names (in case of ICN) to facilitate the communication between the participating networks. Moreover, even when both the Internet and *Sensor Networks* run the same protocol, *e.g.*, ICN, *FOGG* will support the mapping of the lengthy, unbounded names that could be used in the Internet operating with an ICN protocol such as NDN to their equivalent short names in the *Sensor Networks* operating with a lighter version of ICN such as the CCN-lite protocol. It is clear that since the IPv6 MTU is 1280B while the IEEE 802.15.4 can support only 127B, the authors in the IETF standard [18] suggest that header compression in IPv6 is unavoidable. However, the content generated in the *Sensor Network* is assumed to be small. *FOGG* could therefore play an active role in header compression too.

5.3.3 Communication techniques

There are two important modes of communication in the Internet and IoT: Query/Response (Q/R) and Publish/Subscribe (pub/sub). The *Fog Gateway* can support both forms of communications. For Q/R the *Fog Gateway* will perform the protocol translation between Internet protocol like NDN to the CCN-lite protocol in *Sensor Networks*. Whereas for pub/sub, the *Fog Gateway* can assist in maintaining long term subscriptions. When a publication packet reaches the *Fog Gateway* it will perform the protocol translation into respective protocol of the target network and forward the publication packet to the subscribers.

5.3.4 Secure onboarding

The *Fog Gateway* speeds up the deployment of new devices in the *Sensor Network* by automating the configuration to a large extent. The *Fog Gateway* uses a registration procedure for every device in the *Sensor Network* for secure-onboarding. Each sensor device upon entering the *Sensor Network* must register itself with the *Fog Gateway*. The *Fog Gateway* provides an ID to each newly added sensor device. Since in many applications the devices tend to sleep, based on the location of the device, the controller in the *Fog Gateway* sends information about sleeping patterns to the device for configurations to ensure a stable network at all times. This is essential as in a multi-hop network, all the intermediate devices should be awake simultaneously to ensure successful communication. In case of ICN, the sensor device also registers the short name and long name of the content that it wishes to serve. These entries will be added to the mapping table maintained in the *Fog Gateway*. The mapping table should be updated whenever there are any changes in the content served by the sensor devices.

5.3.5 Data: pre-fetching, caching, filtering

Further, the applications interested in the data generated by the sensor devices need
the data to be processed before use. Due to the controller intelligence available at
FOGG, it could proactively pre-fetch and cache content that would be required in
the near future. Further, the *Fog Gateway* could perform complex operations on
the data such as filtering of raw data and storage of the processed data on behalf
of the resource constrained sensor devices. The enormous amount of data produced
by the IoT devices [133] is already a concern for Big Data. However, not all of the
data generated by the sensor devices is important to be transmitted and stored.
e.g., the devices that periodically sense the temperature of an equipment need to
store only the abnormalities. *Fog Gateway* can greatly reduce the required storage
by pre-processing the data to filter only the important data for storage.

5.3.6 Security

Since, security is also a major concern, *FOGG* satisfies this requirement by utilizing
ICN security features which provides data-centric security instead of securing the
end to end communication channel like in IP. If the devices cannot handle the
computational complexity of generating a signature for the content they produce,
during registration the devices can receive a signature from *Fog Gateway* for the
content they produce.

Although we speak about one *Fog Gateway* between the Internet and each *Sensor
Network*, there is no restriction on the number of *Fog Gateways*. As the traffic
exchange between the Internet and *Sensor Networks* increases, the burden on a
single *Fog Gateway* also increases. Hence, multiple *Fog Gateways* have to be used
to form a Fog network and distribute the load.

5.4 Realization of use-cases with FOGG

In this section, we present examples of how *FOGG* could support the various usecases resulting from the scenarios we defined in §5.2.1. Consider the example of a
smart industry with the *FOGG* shown in Figure. 5.2. There is a *Fog Gateway* in
each *Sensor Network* that collects the readings sensed by the devices periodically
every 30mins. The *Fog Gateway* also receives control messages and forwards it to
devices in the *Sensor Network*. Let us assume that the Internet is running on top
of NDN and the IoT network is running on top of CCN-lite. The *Fog Gateway*

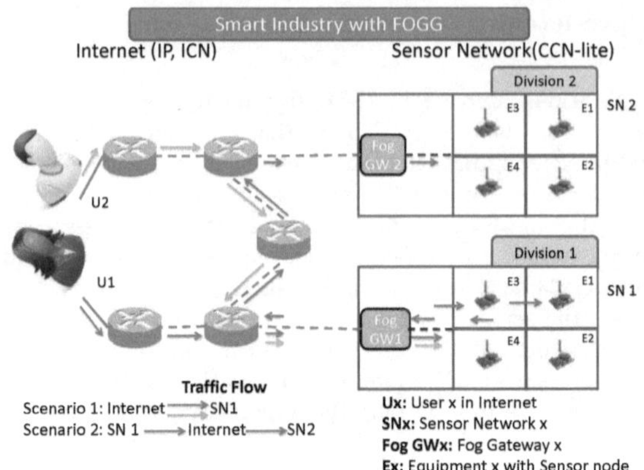

Figure 5.2: **Smart industry use cases with FOGG.**

therefore runs both the NDN and CCN-lite protocols for interconnecting the *Sensor Networks* and the Internet.

5.4.1 Operation

As discussed in Chapter 4, we use the term *Inbound traffic* for the traffic entering the *Sensor Network* and the term *Outbound traffic* for the traffic leaving the *Sensor Network*. The inbound traffic from the users can be either a request for data or a request containing a control message. There are two possible kinds of outbound traffic. One containing the reply to the inbound traffic and the other is the request traffic generated inside the *Sensor Network*. The two types of outbound traffic should be distinguished from one another as the reply traffic needs a name change through a mapping table lookup. This can be easily achieved by using any one bit available field in the packets.

When the *Fog Gateway* receives inbound traffic it is basically a NDN Interest packet. The *Fog Gateway* scans the mapping table to find the equivalent short name. Since the *Fog Gateway* periodically collects the data from the sensing devices, the *Fog Gateway* checks if it already has the data and returns the data if available. Otherwise, the *Fog Gateway* creates a CCN-lite Interest packet with the short name and forwards it to the *Sensor Network*. Upon receiving a CCN-lite Data packet from the *Sensor Network*, the *Fog Gateway* performs a lookup in the mapping table to find the equivalent long name and creates a NDN Data packet with the long name, extracts the content from the CCN-lite Data packet and inserts it into the NDN Data packet and forwards it in the Internet. In case of the outbound traffic generated inside the *Sensor Network*, the *Fog Gateway* merely performs a protocol translation by generating a NDN Interest with the same *content name* as in the CCN-lite Interest. Upon receiving the data it converts it to a CCN-lite Data packet and forwards it to the *Sensor Network*.

5.4.2 Example of *FOGG* with caching and periodic-fetching

A user (U1) in the Internet is interested in the temperature of equipment1 in the division1 at 12:30. So, U1 will generate an NDN Interest with the long name *e.g.*, */temperature/industry/building1/division1/equipment1/16-5-17/12:30*. The network will forward the Interest to Fog Gateway1 (FGW1). FGW1 will check its mapping table for the name. When no match is found, the FGW1 behaves like a router and the NDN module running inside the FGW1 will forward it to the appropriate router in the Internet. If there is a match, since FGW1 periodically collects all the data, if the FGW1 has the content then it will generate the NDN data with the requested content and forward it to the Internet. Otherwise, it generates a CCN-lite Interest with the equivalent short name *e.g.*, */temp/b1/d1/e1/16-5-17/12:30* and forwards it to the device E1 in the *Sensor Network1*. Upon receiving a CCN-lite data, the *Fog Gateway* will scan its mapping table to find the short name. If there is a match, the FGW1 will extract the content from the CCN-lite Data packet, generate an NDN Data packet with the equivalent long name with the extracted content and forward it to the Internet. When there is no match found in the mapping table the FGW1 will discard the Data packet.

5.4.3 Example of *FOGG* performing protocol translation

The sensor device E3 in the SN1 needs the viscocity of the liquid it boils from the sensor device E3 in SN2 operating in division2. It generates a CCN-lite Interest with the long name *e.g.*, */viscocity/industry/building2/division2/equipment3* and forwards it to FGW1. Please note that since this is an outbound traffic for content located outside the *Sensor Network* this should be indicated by setting any available bit in the Interest packet. For CCN-lite the EXCLUDE field can be used to indicate this. Upon receiving this Interest, the FGW1 identifies it as an outbound traffic by inspecting the one bit field. The *Fog Gateway* will only perform a protocol translation by generating an NDN Interest with the same name and forward it to the Internet. The content may be located in the Internet or also in another *Sensor Network*. The producer either from the Internet or any other *Sensor Network* will reply with the content. Upon receiving a Data packet the FGW1 will again perform a protocol translation by extracting the content from the NDN Data packet and generate the CCN-lite Data packet with the content and forward it to E3.

5.4.4 Example of *FOGG* performing pre-filtering

All the sensor devices in the *Sensor Network* 1 & 2 sense some data and send this raw data immediately to the *Fog Gateway*. The *Fog Gateway* filters the raw data and performs the necessary computations desired by the application that uses this data. If abnormalities are identified, the *Fog Gateway* immediately notifies the administrator and raises an alarm in case of emergencies like fire.

5.4.5 Example of *FOGG* performing controlling

An equipment E2 in division1 has an actuator connected to it which opens and closes the lid for controlling the air pressure inside the equipment. The sensor device attached to E2 sends periodic readings of the pressure to *Fog Gateway* for monitoring. The *Fog Gateway* monitors the reading and when the readings are above a threshold, the *Fog Gateway* sends a control message to the actuator fitted with the E2 to open the lid for exact amount of time computed by *Fog Gateway*. The actuator upon receiving the control message performs the required operation and sends an acknowledgement of the action performed. If the action was unsuccessful, the *Fog Gateway* will notify the administrator as a technical error has occurred and a human intervention is necessary to avoid risks.

5.5 Chapter summary

In this chapter, we discussed the shortcomings of current IoT designs and introduced Fog computing with ICN. We observed that ICN is more suitable for supporting IoT compared to IP in Chapter 4 and proposed the *ISI* architecture to integrate *Sensor Networks* to the Internet. In this Chapter, we utilized the *ISI* architecture and leveraged the benefits of Fog computing to realize a Fog computing based Gateway. We analyzed the various requirements to integrate the *Sensor Networks* and proposed *FOGG* with *Fog Gateways*. We described in detail the responsibilities of such a *Fog Gateway* and further described the communication protocol for IoT networks. With the help of use cases we described the functionality of *FOGG* and showed the benefits of such a Gateway to realize IoT.

Chapter 6

COPSS-lite: A Lightweight ICN based Pub/Sub System for IoT Environments

Traditional query/response based communication establishes point-point connection for data exchange. However, this limits the possibility of obtaining content available at multiple different sources. Moreover, the receivers are expected to know in advance when the content is generated in order to request the content. Therefore, in recent years, publish/subscribe (pub/sub) systems have gained popularity as they dismiss the need for users to request every content of their interest. Instead, the content is supplied to the interested users (subscribers) as and when it is published by the producers. CCN/NDN [6] are popular ICN proposals that are widely accepted in the ICN community; however, they do not provide an efficient pub/sub mechanism. Hence, a content oriented pub/sub system named COPSS [3] was developed to enhance the CCN/NDN protocols with efficient pub/sub capabilities. Internet houses powerful devices like routers and servers that can operate with the full-fledged implementation of such ICN protocols. However, Internet of Things (IoT) has become a growing topic of interest in recent years with billions of resource constrained devices expected to connect to the Internet in the near future to realize many emerging new applications. The current design to support IoT relies mainly on IP which has limited address space and hence cannot accommodate the increasing number of devices. Even though, IPv6 provides a large address space, IoT devices operate with constrained resources and hence, IPv6 protocol and its headers will induce additional overhead for their operation. Interestingly, we observed that IoTs are information centric in nature and therefore, ICN could be a more suitable candidate to support IoT environments. Although NDN and COPSS are designed for the Internet, their current full fledged implementations cannot be used by the resource constrained IoT devices. Therefore, CCN-lite [20] was designed to provide a light weight, inter-operable version of the CCNx protocol to support the IoT devices. However, CCN-lite like its ancestors (CCN/NDN) lacks the support for an efficient pub/sub mechanism. Therefore, in this chapter, we develop *COPSS-lite*, an efficient and light weight implementation of pub/sub to support the information centric IoT networks. Essentially, *COPSS-lite* enhances CCN-lite with pub/sub capability with minimal overhead and further enables multi-hop connections by incorporating the popular RPL [134] protocol for low power and lossy networks. This chapter also provides evaluations using the real world sensor devices from the IoT Lab, to demonstrate the benefits of *COPSS-lite* in comparison with stand alone CCN-lite. Our results show that *COPSS-lite* is compact, operates on all platforms that support CCN-lite and significantly improves the performance of constrained devices in the IoT environments.

The key contributions in this work include:

- Analysis of the requirements of IoT environments.
- *COPSS-lite*: enhancements to the initial COPSS design to support IoT environments.
- Incorporating *COPSS-lite* with CCN-lite to provide efficient pub/sub capability to CCN-lite.
- A prototype of *COPSS-lite* developed in the IoT lab[2] using real sensor devices on RIOT[3] OS.
- Evaluation to demonstrate the benefits offered by *COPSS-lite*.

Contents

6.1 ICN architecture

In this section, we briefly describe the ICN proposals that necessitated the need for proposing *COPSS-lite* for the IoT environments.

6.1.1 CCN-lite

The CCN-lite [20] project is a step towards supporting resource constrained devices to leverage the benefits provided by ICN protocols. CCN-lite is essentially a light weight implementation of the CCN [6] protocol resulting from the project. The rationale for developing CCN-lite was by 2011, PARC's CCNx routers had acquired wide acceptance and were growing in popularity. The CCN-lite project aimed at designing a lighter version to mainly support educational needs and experiments without needing the full fledged implementation of the complete CCNx protocol and all its features.

CCN-lite is an inter-operable implementation of the CCNx and NDN protocol that supports CCN, NDN, Named Function Networking (NFN [135]) and IoT. Essentially, CCN-lite provides the core CCNx functionalities with less than 2000 lines of code in C language and hence it has a low memory footprint. It supports multiple platforms like Linux, Android, Arduino, RFduino and OMNET++. Further, RIOT the free, open source operating system designed especially for IoT has incorporated CCN-lite in its implementation to allow various IoT devices to run ICN protocols.

6.1.2 COPSS

As explained in Chapter 2, COPSS adds a Subscription Table (ST) to the initial CCN forwarding engine. Every COPSS router maintains a ST for enabling the pub/sub communication in a distributed and aggregated manner. COPSS also introduces two new packet types: *Subscribe* and *Publish* to enable pub/sub in ICN. Unlike NDN, COPSS uses Content Descriptors (CD) which are essentially some features of the content like keywords, date of publication, identity of the publisher, *etc.* as content identifiers for managing the pub/sub communication. The Subscribe packet is used by the users to subscribe to a certain CD while the Publish packet is used by the publisher to publish the content for a single or group of CD's *i.e.*, a piece of content can be associated with multiple CD's. Each CD is assigned to a respective Rendezvous Point (RP) node in the network.

At the onset of the pub/sub communication, subscribers will subscribe to the content of their interest by subscribing to the associated CD's, resulting in a join. When a router receives a subscription request, it adds an entry in its ST with the CD and the incoming face of the request and subsequently forwards the request upstream towards the RP. The intermediate routers also add an entry for the subscription in their ST and forward the subscription packet towards the designated RP for the CD(s) in the subscription packet. When the publisher generates any content, (s)he associates the content with their respective CD(s). Whenever the content is published, it travels along the multicast tree towards the responsible RP. When a router receives a publication packet, it checks the ST for any one of the CD's in the publication. If a match is found then the router forwards the publication packet along the matched interfaces. However, only a single copy of the publication is forwarded on each interface, irrespective of the number of subscribers in the downstream. This avoids, unnecessary traffic and duplicate/multiple copies delivered to the subscribers of more than one CD in the publication packet.

6.2 IoT requirements

IoT environment allows numerous physical devices in the sensor networks to integrate with the Internet. Such an integration of the physical world into the software based Internet enables the possibility to expedite automation in many areas. The design of IoT environments varies greatly compared to the design of the Internet irrespective of the traditional IP or the ICN based networks. The nature of the devices operating in the IoT environment is also very different and especially constrained in resources like computational capacity, memory, power, *etc.* Even though, the IP based designs are emerging for supporting the IoT networks, in PHOENIX, we argue that IoT environments are content centric in nature and hence, ICN based solutions are more suitable for IoT networks. We therefore identify the following important requirements that should be met by the underlying network protocol for efficiently supporting the IoT environments.

Communication Protocol: In an IoT environment, since most of the IoT application tend to operate in a publish/subscribe fashion the pull based mechanism to retrieve the data can turn out to be a huge disadvantage especially in terms of the network load, processing capacity and power consumption. It is desired for the underlying network to provide an efficient platform for pub/sub to enable these devices to operate optimally.

Timeliness: Many IoT applications are sensitive to time *e.g.*, emergency applications, environmental monitoring, disaster notifications, industrial alarming systems, *etc.* Hence, the underlying communication protocol should be reactive and must ensure a timely delivery of the messages for latency sensitive applications in the IoT environment.

Power Consumption: Many IoT devices operate with limited power supply, mostly a battery. Some devices are expected to operate in remote locations without any human intervention/supervision for longer periods of time. Hence, it is crucial for these devices to save power to increase their operational life time. Many devices also tend to sleep during most of their life to save power. The underlying network protocol should support such behaviour and efficiently form the network with available devices and ensure connectivity and data availability at all times.

6.3 *COPSS-lite* architecture

In this chapter, we designed *COPSS-lite* mainly to support the IoT environments. The IoT environments are usually composed of hybrid devices that mostly sense and produce data of interest for applications that intent to gather, control or monitor the sensed data. The IoT devices tend to operate in a pub/sub paradigm where we can identify the various sensor devices that periodically sense some data as the publishers. While the nodes, usually Base Stations (Sinks) are interested in receiving such data as the subscribers. A reverse scenario is where a Base Station Controller (BSC) sends some messages/instructions to control the operation of other devices in the network. In this scenario, the BSC behaves like a publisher while the devices that receive the control messages and act on it behave like the subscribers.

The pub/sub models are very popular in the prevailing IP based Internet. However, the current pub/sub systems in the Internet are supported mainly via the client side applications and servers to deliver the published content to the subscribers. This entails additional responsibility/burden for the IP based solutions. In [66, 67] authors show that IP based solutions tend to waste network resources. Hence a content-oriented pub/sub system like COPSS is necessary to enhance the initial design of CCN by integrating it with an efficient and scalable pub/sub capability not only for the devices in Internet but also for the IoT environments (*COPSS-lite*).

We discern that most of the IoT devices are heavily constrained in their avail-

Table 6.1: **Code size estimations.**

RIOT	51540 KB
CCN-lite	18212 KB
COPSS-lite	192 kB

able resources compared to their Internet counterparts. *COPSS-lite* architecture is designed to add the IoT related enhancements to the original COPSS architecture. Thereby, *COPSS-lite* adds an efficient pub/sub model to the CCN-lite protocol for IoT environments. *COPSS-lite* also aims to add several additional features that can support the resource constrained IoT devices. One of the main requirement we identified is the timely delivery of the information without cutting down the operational lifetime of the devices. Therefore, *COPSS-lite* proposes to use the pub/sub communication model to reduce the latency of information retrieval (see §6.5) compared to the pull based mechanism in CCN-lite. To support the other important requirement of reducing the power consumption we develop *COPSS-lite* as a compact version of COPSS with CCN-lite. CCN-lite is currently implemented using UDP or TCP encapsulation for exchanging the CCN-lite packets. The *COPSS-lite* implementation is written purely in C and hence, it is backward compatible with the CCN-lite code. We understand that having a smaller code base is necessary for the IoT devices and can greatly benefit not only in reducing the consumption of power but also in terms of memory and reduced computational overhead. Hence, *COPSS-lite* adds only 334 lines of code to the original CCN-lite code base to provide the necessary functionalities for pub/sub (necessary details are shown in the Table 6.1).

Since many IoT devices show an inclination towards sleeping, it raises a concern on the effective placement of the RP. Since RP is crucial to enable the pub/sub communication in *COPSS-lite*, we believe the need to identify the responsible node is imminent. However, there is no one best answer to this question as the nature of sensor networks varies greatly from one application to another. We believe that pointing out the need is essential. Therefore, we suggest to assign RP to nodes that are either awake all the time (enabled with continuous power supply) or if they are awake when any other node is awake in the network. The selection of the RP node in an IoT network should ensure that RP is reachable by any node that is awake in the network.

Further, an effective pub/sub solution should also address the necessity to limit data loss, especially in a network where most of the nodes are sleeping and hence not operational at all times. We propose to utilize a powerful node like the *ISI* Gateway from Chapter 4 or to equip the sensor networks with a controller node similar to Software Defined Networking (SDN). The controller maintains information about all the devices in its sensor network. The controller node is aware of the sleeping pattern of the devices and hence can efficiently create ad-hoc networks. Such a network will allow reactive forwarding of the content effectively utilizing the network and ensures maximum packet transmission with minimal loss. The controller also stores the state information of all the nodes like their ST, and computes routing tables (FIB) for the current duration. The controller can also store the publications while the nodes are sleeping and propagate it when the nodes wake-up. Every node has a logical one-hop connection to the controller. Whenever a node wakes up it contacts the controller and retrieves its state information and joins the network. Once the network is created, the messages can flow seamlessly.

A two-step communication process in COPSS allows the publisher to exercise control over the access and policy of the published contents. In a two-step communication process, the publishers generate a snippet of the original content with the associated CD's and send it to the subscribers. Interested subscribers can then use these CD's to subscribe to the full-length original content. The publishers then publish the original content which is forwarded to the interested subscribers as explained previously. Similarly, *COPSS-lite* also provides the two-step communication process for the IoT environment. Whenever a new device joins the network, it can send a snippet of the data that it wishes to publish along with the CD's to the controller. The controller will disseminate the publication advertisement in the network and the interested users can subscribe to it. The controller in *COPSS-lite* ensures minimum overhead on the constrained devices, minimizes loss of publications/subscriptions and maximizes the utilization of the network.

6.4 Implementation

6.4.1 CCN-lite with RIOT OS

The RIOT networking interface follows the GNRC network stack. The entire implementation runs on link layer. The RIOT OS has incorporated the CCN-lite features on to its OS by building a dedicated RIOT-CCN adapter. The adapter integrates CCN-lite with RIOT and creates a loop back interface between the RIOT network interface and the CCN-lite code. During operation, all the GNRC packets are first forwarded to the RIOT-CCN adapter. If the adapter finds that packets have arrived from the GNRC link layer or from the CCN-lite callback, it parses the GNRC packets to CCN-lite packets and forwards them to CCN-lite via the callback interface. Upon processing, CCN-lite forwards the packets to the outside network or to the local RIOT application. Whereas, if the packets arrived from local applications,

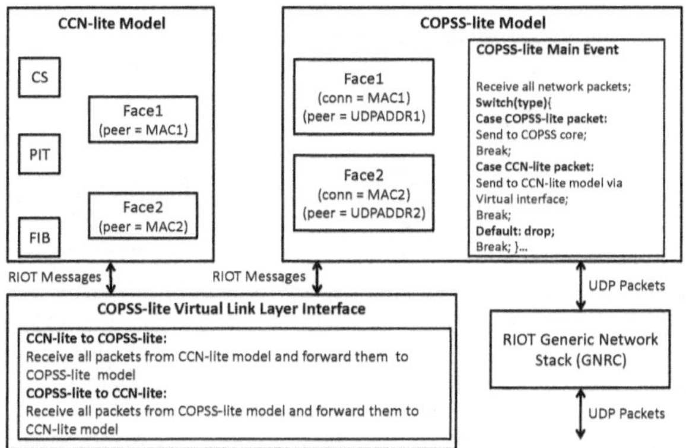

Figure 6.1: **Components and message exchange.**

then CCN-lite receives the packets via the adapter interface, processes the packets and sends them back. The packets are parsed to GNRC packets and then forwarded to the outside network.

6.4.2 Challenges

Even though our choice for OS (RIOT) [136] and CCN (CCN-lite) implementation were clear, developing *COPSS-lite* from COPSS was not straight forward. We faced several challenges mainly:

- CCN-lite works with RIOT on layer 2, whereas COPSS was implemented to work in transport layer with UDP.
- IoT networks are unstable and need multi-hop routing support without any layer 3 devices.
- CCN-lite has reduced some original features of NDN that are needed in COPSS like registering prefixes, *etc*.

6.4.3 Design

We developed *COPSS-lite* with the latest versions of RIOT OS, CCN-lite and the GCC compiler (details are shown in Table 6.2(a)). In *COPSS-lite*, we use the

Table 6.2: **Development platform and hardware details.**

(a) Development platform

OS	RIOT,Linux
ICN	CCN-lite0.3.0
Compiler	GCC4.8.4
Hardware	M3,A8

(b) M3 and A8 node

MCU	ARM CORTEX M3, 32-bits
Radio	802.15.4
Power	3.7VLiPo battery
OS	M3{FreeRTOS, Contiki, RIOT} A8{Linux}
ICN	CCN-lite

Type-Length-Value format for the subscription and publication packets to ensure compatibility and consistency with CCN-lite implementation on RIOT. Further, we developed a design that loosely couples the interaction of CCN-lite and *COPSS-lite* models with the underlying RIOT system.

Figure 6.1 shows the components and the message exchange between CCN-lite, RIOT and *COPSS-lite*. We add an intermediate layer called *COPSS-lite Virtual Interface* to build a bridge between the CCN-lite and *COPSS-lite* models. The CCN-lite module refers to the current CCN-lite implementation in RIOT while the *COPSS-lite* module refers to the implemented *COPSS-lite* logic. The *COPSS-lite* virtual link layer interface is the adapter between the CCN-lite and *COPSS-lite*. The CCN-lite works on the link layer in RIOT and the packets are transmitted using the MAC addresses. In the *COPSS-lite* component, each time a user creates a face, the *COPSS-lite* creates an associating face in CCN-lite and assigns a unique virtual MAC address to it. The *COPSS-lite* virtual link layer interface is created to replace the default RIOT link layer interface for CCN-lite so that the CCN-lite packets will be forwarded to the *COPSS-lite* virtual interface instead. *COPSS-lite* module is the main pub/sub component added by the *COPSS-lite* implementation. The *COPSS-lite* module has one main thread and two sub modules: *COPSS-lite* core and *COPSS-lite* forwarder. The Main thread receives all the packets and determines which submodule should process the packet. The *COPSS-lite* module deals with the subscribe and publish packets while the *COPSS-lite* forwarder forwards the CCN-lite Interest and Data packets to the CCN-lite module via the *COPSS-lite* virtual link layer interface.

6.5 Evaluation

To evaluate the performance of *COPSS-lite*, we used real sensor devices in the IoT Lab[4] to conduct our tests. IoT lab provides a large scale infrastructure facility

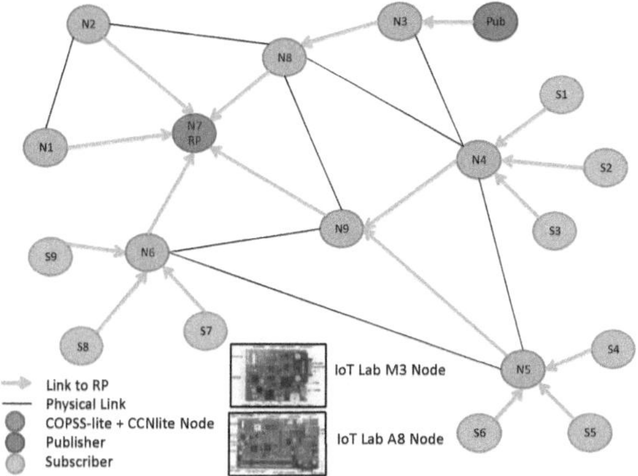

Figure 6.2: **Topology.**

with real sensor devices for experimentation. It offers three development boards for experimentation: WSN430, M3 and A8 nodes. We used the M3 and A8 nodes to run our evaluations as they offer a 32-bit system and support CCN-lite (WSN430 is 16-bit). The development platform and hardware specifications are shown in Table 6.2(b). Figure 6.2 shows the multi-hop topology used for evaluation. In this evaluation, we measure the aggregated network load and latency experienced by the users with pub/sub in *COPSS-lite* and query/response in CCN-lite.

We comprehend that there are numerous different IoT applications, each with their own respective traffic pattern. Hence, we determined that it would be reasonable to test with different distributions that mimic the traffic pattern in the IoT environments. We used the popular distributions of Zipf, Geometric, Uniform and Binomial to represent the various traffic patterns in the IoT environments for the evaluation. The Zipf distribution shows that most popular content with the highest rank is published more often than the content with the lower ranks. Whereas, in the Geometric distribution, the probability sequence for publishing a piece of content follows a geometric sequence. The Uniform distribution shows a traffic pattern with constant probability for publishing the content. While the Binomial distribution shows the number of success in n independent trails with the probability of p. Further, we generated a small dataset with 10 different kinds of content to mimic the data generated by the sensor devices. As shown in the topology in Figure 6.2, we configured nine nodes to run the CCN-lite and *COPSS-lite* software with the RIOT OS. For the experiments, we increased the number of subscribers starting form 1 to 9 with a single producer who published the content.

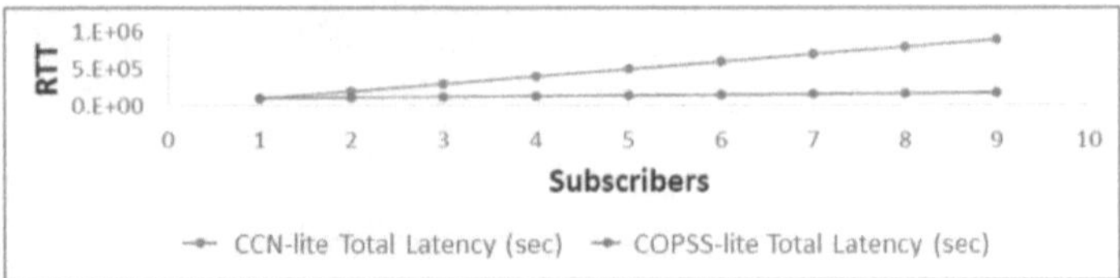

Figure 6.3: **Latency in seconds.**

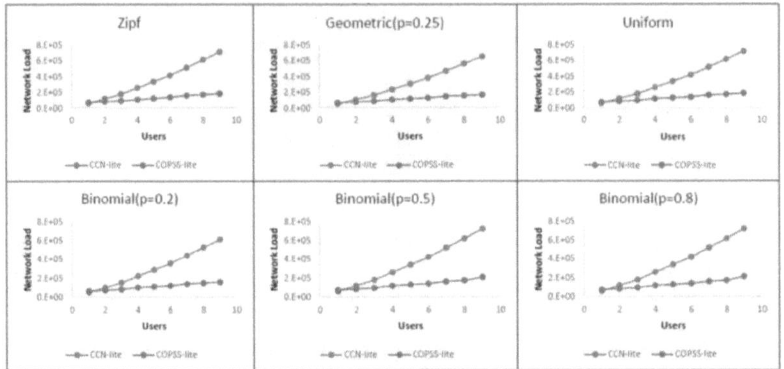

Figure 6.4: **Network load with different traffic patterns.**

To test the effectiveness, we published the data with Zipf, Geometric (p=0.25), Uniform and Binomial (p= 0.2, 0.5, and 0.8) distributions. The resulting latency experienced by the user is shown in Figure 6.3 and the corresponding network load is shown in the Figure 6.4. We observe from the results that network load an latency experienced by the users are significantly less in IoT environment with the pub/sub based *COPSS-lite* system compared to the query/response based CCN-lite system. Hence, we conclude that *COPSS-lite* based IoT devices operate efficiently and optimally with their constrained resources in the ICN environment.

6.6 Chapter summary

In this chapter, we focussed on the IoT environments highlighting their imminent growth in the near future. We discussed the potential problems that resource con-

strained IoT devices face with IP and emphasized the inherent content centric nature
of the IoT environments and subsequently, suggested ICN for supporting IoT environments. We then discussed CCN-lite which provides just enough features to
run the ICN protocol in IoT environments. However, we studied that CCN-lite
like its predecessors does not provide an efficient pub/sub mechanism for the IoT
environments. Moreover, we observed that pub/sub is the more preferred communication protocol in IoT environments. Hence, we developed *COPSS-lite*, a light-
weight, inter-operable version of pub/sub for IoT and incorporated it with CCN-
lite. Additionally, with real world sensor devices from the IoT Lab we evaluated the
performance of *COPSS-lite* and showed that IoT devices can greatly benefit with
COPSS-lite.

Chapter 7

NeMoI: Network Mobility in ICN

With the advancement in technology, mobility has become a norm. Recent trend towards 5G and increasing popularity of IoT is expected to demand increased mobility support in the network. ICN treats content as the first class entity and nodes exchange information based on the identity of the content rather than the location of the content. ICN inherently supports consumer mobility and there are many recent works on producer mobility. However, an untouched area of work is ICN's support for network mobility. Network-segments/domains comprising of various networking nodes, consumers and producers can also experience mobility and can aggravate the problems associated with supporting mobility. This chapter proposes *NeMoI: Network Mobility in ICN*, a full fledged ICN based mobility solution with a special focus on network mobility including the case of producers and consumers present within such mobile networks.

The key contributions in this work include:

- An enhanced architecture to support network-on-the-move in ICN.
- Distributed Mobility Agents service for name resolution.
- A distributed deployment model for realizing Mobility Agents.
- A new field "Time Stamp" in the Binding Interest packet.
- Logically multi-layered Forwarding Information Base.
- Proactive and Reactive solutions to synchronize mobility updates.
- Enhanced Security features.

Contents

7.1 Scenario and Objectives

7.1.1 Mobility scenario

Let us consider a scenario where a person P has a mobile phone and is walking towards a train station. If P uses his/her phone to watch a video or read some news, then he/she becomes a consumer of that content. Whereas if P is uploads some photos/videos or any other type of content then P becomes the producer of that respective content. Once P reaches the train station, he/she decides to board a train and subsequently connect to the WiFi access point available in the train. When the train starts to move, it represents a network-on-the-move. Further, during the journey, P can change the train resulting in a shift from one network-on-the-move to another. Let us also consider a nested network-on-the-move scenario where P is in a moving train and he/she is using the Internet by connecting to the WiFi in the train. P decides to connect his laptop to the Internet via the mobile phone which is already connected to the WiFi access point in the train. In this scenario, mobility will trigger updates from all the connected devices, and thereby, escalating the problem. In the near future, especially with increasing popularity of IoT and 5G, we believe such mobility will most likely be a norm and is a matter of concern that demands attention.

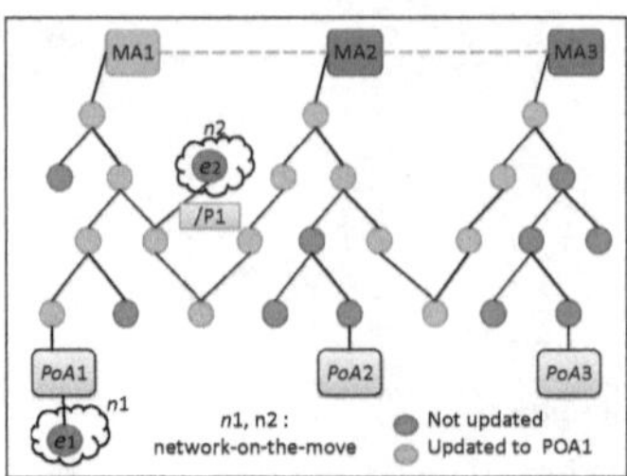

Figure 7.1: **First mobility update.**

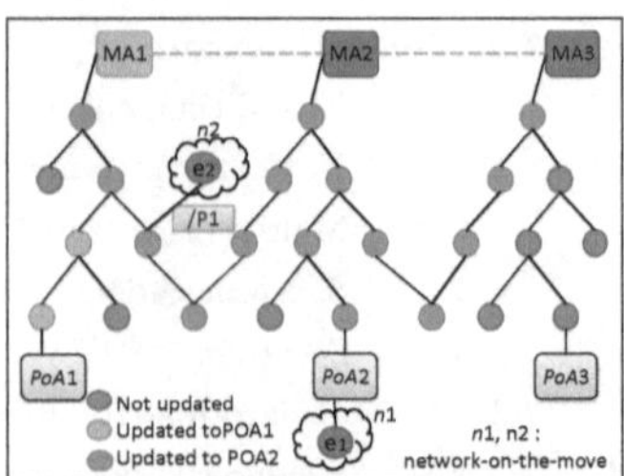

Figure 7.2: **Second mobility update.**

7.1.2 Objectives

Based on the above mobility scenario, we derive the following objectives that should be met by a mobility solution in ICN.

Mobility support: There are basically three kinds of mobility: consumer, producer and network-on-the-move. An efficient mobility solution should support all three kinds of mobility.

Synchronization: The solution should ensure that mobility updates are synchronized in the network especially with the previous location of the mobile entity.

Signalling traffic: Increased mobility will cause signalling traffic to consume majority of the traffic in the network. The solution should try to minimize such signalling traffic.

Mobility update: Mobility updates should be propagated throughout the network. However, the updates should not overwhelm the network especially with continuous mobility. A routers main task is to forward request/data traffic, hence, routers should not be overloaded with control traffic and frequent updates to their routing tables.

Path Inflation: The solution should try to minimize the path inflation experienced by users due to mobility.

Packet Loss: The solution should try to minimize the packet loss experienced by users due to mobility.

7.2 NeMoI: design

A mobility solution should meet certain objectives like, supporting consumer, producer and network-on-the-move mobility, synchronize mobility updates, minimize signalling traffic, routing updates, path inflation and packet loss experienced by consumers. In this section, we describe the design of NeMoI architecture with the topology in Figure 7.1 and show how NeMoI meets these objectives.

7.2.1 NeMoI components

End-point: The term end-point is used to refer to any end-user/IoT node that attaches to the network. The end-point can be within network-on-the-move or static. It can represent consumers and producers. Figure 7.1 shows some end-points in a network-on-the-move.

Point of Attachment (*PoA*): They are the dedicated nodes in the network that end points use to connect to the network *i.e.* the access routers. Figure 1a shows three such *PoA*s. In NeMoI, every *PoA* has an ICN routable name, e.g. *PoA*1.

Mobility Agent (*MA*): The network is composed of numerous Mobility Agents. Figure 7.1 shows three *MA*s in the sample topology. Every *MA* is responsible for maintaining information about the current location of the producer(s) associated with the *MA* and resolve the prefixes in the received *Interest*s. Similar to *PoA* every *MA* also has an ICN routable name *e.g.*, *MA*1.

Domain/Network Segment: A network segment[5] is basically a small part of the original network composed of numerous networking nodes, consumers and producers. *E.g.*, the moving network *n1* with end-point *e1* in Figure 7.1. Every domain is capable of mobility and must ensure connectivity to nodes located in the domain with the rest of the network.

Binding Interest: We introduce a logical packet type called *Binding Interest* (BI) shown in Figure 7.4 to propagate mobility update information in the network. For implementation, *Interest* packets could be enhanced with the fields in Figure 7.4 to function as mobility update packets.

7.2.2 NeMoI architecture

7.2.2.1 Mobility agents

Many anchor based (See §2.2.4) solutions [22, 26, 103] use Home Agents to support producer mobility. Similarly, NeMoI proposes Mobility Agents (*MAs*) to assist in both network-on-the-move and end-point mobility in ICN. Despite various anchorless proposals for source mobility, we realized that dedicated nodes to perform name

---

[5]*Domain & network segment* is used interchangeably in this chapter.

Primary Table	
Prefix	Routable component
/p1	/n1
/t1	PoA1

Secondary Table	
Prefix	Routable component
/a	/n2

Producer e1: /p1/sports   **prefix:**/p1
Network-segment n1 :/n1/network_profile   **prefix:**/n1
routable component for e1 **in** n1: /n1

Figure 7.3: **Mobility Agent tables.**

resolution for mobile nodes can increase reliability and robustness of the network. We however, provide optimization techniques to increase the propagation of mobility updates and by pass the *MAs*. Therefore, NeMoI is in fact a hybrid solution.

In NeMoI, a *MA* is a normal ICN forwarder with added functionality of NeMoI and has a routable name *e.g.*, MA1. The *MAs* are deployed in a distributed manner in the network. Each *MA* is responsible for resolving a set of primary prefixes and a set of secondary prefixes served by the producers. For reliability and robustness, the primary *MA* is a logical *MA*, while one or more physical *MAs* can share the associated tasks. The *MAs* maintain two tables, a primary table containing all the primary prefixes and their current location and a secondary table containing all the secondary prefixes and their current location. Figure 7.3 shows the internal structure of a *MA* where a producer p1 generates a content with the prefix /p and is located in a network-segment identified with the prefix /n1. Hence, /n1 is used as a routable component to reach p1. The figure also shows the secondary table for the prefix /a for which this *MA* is a secondary *MA*. As shown in Figure 7.1 the *MAs* maintain a logical one-hop connection with their neighbouring *MAs* in the network forming an overlay network for synchronizing the mobility updates. For load balancing *MAs* can drop some of their secondary prefixes.

The functionality of *MAs* is provided as a network service and it is managed by the network administrators. Based on our study, we provide the following two different options for realizing the *MAs* service.

- **Option1:** There are numerous *MAs* in the network, each tasked with managing a set of dedicated prefixes. When a new *MA* needs to be added to this overlay network, the network administrator identifies a network node and configures the *MA* on it. As part of the configuration, the network administrator assigns a name to the *MA*, its neighbouring *MAs* and the set of primary and secondary prefixes that this *MA* is responsible for resolving. The administrator also modifies the neighbours list of the respective *MAs* that are neighbours of the newly added *MA*. Similar to the producers, the newly added *MA* will leverage the NDN routing protocol such as NLSR to inform the routers of its presence.

Every router that receives the update from the newly added *MA* can check the number of hops to this *MA* and decide if it is in its shortest path and add it to its routing table before forwarding it to its neighbours. If the *MA* is not in the shortest path, then the update will be discarded. Similarly, when a *MA* is removed from a router, the network administrator assigns the prefixes (if required) to other *MAs* and update the neighbour list of the affected *MAs*. The affected *MAs* use the NDN routing protocols to inform the changes by indicating the name of the *MA* that has been removed. The routers that receive this information can check if their shortest path *MA* is in the list of removed *MA*, if yes then they update their routing information.

- **Option 2:** The *MAs* can be realized as a network service with a single *MA* that is implemented with distributed servers in the network. Where the network has numerous dedicated nodes configured to function as *MAs*. This is again a overlay network, where the *MAs* communicate with each other and synchronize the mobility update. The difference from the first option is that all the *MAs* will store the record for all the prefixes, similar to DNS servers. This type of service may incur influx of updates to some servers while others remain idle, and hence a load balancing mechanism needs to be in place, but this is out of scope of this chapter.

In this chapter, we will refer to the first design while describing the functionality of NeMoI. It is possible for the *MAs* to fail due to various reasons e.g., hardware failure, crash due to increased load, etc. However, since the *MA* is a service that is managed separately by the network administrator, there are several possibilities for recovery. Like instantiating the service on a new node in the network and updating the existing *MAs* with this information. However, there is a need to transfer the states from the crashed *MA* to the newly instantiated *MA*. One possible solution is for the *MAs* to periodically store a snapshot of their states in a server that is administered by the network administrator. The newly instantiated *MA* can then be initialized with the state information of the crashed *MA*.

The allocation of prefixes to *MAs* can be achieved by network administrators or a dedicated Registrar responsible for allocating unique prefixes to producers. At the time of allocating prefixes, the respective *MA* can also be allocated. The *MAs* can delegate prefixes to one another or decide to be in synchronization for a set of prefixes. We only provide some suggestion about the allocation of prefixes to *MAs* in this chapter.

Prefix (s)
Routable Component
Sequence No.
Time Stamp

Reverse Update	Reverse Update Received
Old Routable Component	
Signature	

Figure 7.4: **Binding *Interest* packet.**

Content Name
Routable Component
Selector (order preference, publisher filter, scope,...)
Signature

Figure 7.5: **CCN *Interest* with Routable Component.**

7.2.2.2 Binding Interest

In order to carry out the mobility updates we introduce a new packet type called the *Binding Interest* (*BI*) in NeMoI as shown in the Figure 7.4 . The first field in the BI is used to specify one or more *Prefix* served by the producer. The second field specifies the *routable component* that can be used to reach the producer at the new location. The *routable component* is basically the name of the new *PoA* in the network. The third field is the *Sequence Number* used to distinguish between multiple mobility updates generated during continuous mobility *e.g.*, during a train journey. It is the responsibility of the mobile node to increment the sequence number in every new BI forwarded in the network. The fourth field is the *Time Stamp*, which indicates the duration for which the *routable component* is valid for routing. This is set by the mobile entity and stored in both the *MAs* tables and in the FIB. This field is added to prevent the reuse of out-dated routing components and to maintain a clean FIB and *MAs* record. However, this necessitates that all the entities that use the time stamp should have an accurate clock for synchronization. Therefore, in NeMoI, we suggest the participating entities to utilize the Network Time Protocol [137] to synchronize their clocks. The next two fields namely, *Reverse Update* (*RU*) and *Reverse Update Received* (*RUR*) are used to update the old location about the new *PoA*. While the following field contains the old *routable component* used to reach the previous *PoA*. The last field contains the *Signature* of the mobile node that generated the BI.

Every producer in the network is associated to at least one logical primary *MA* and many secondary *MAs*. Every *PoA* in the network has a routable name *e.g.*, *PoA*1. Whenever a producer moves to a new location and attaches to a *PoA* in the network, the producer can obtain the name of the *PoA* similar to obtaining access point names in IP. The producer then sends a *Binding Interest* (*BI*) containing the prefixes served

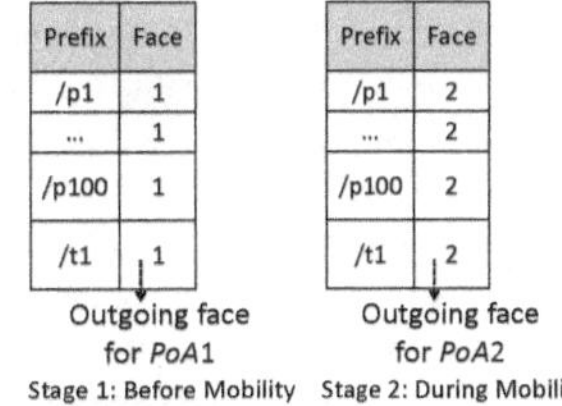

Figure 7.6: **FIB with no indirection.**

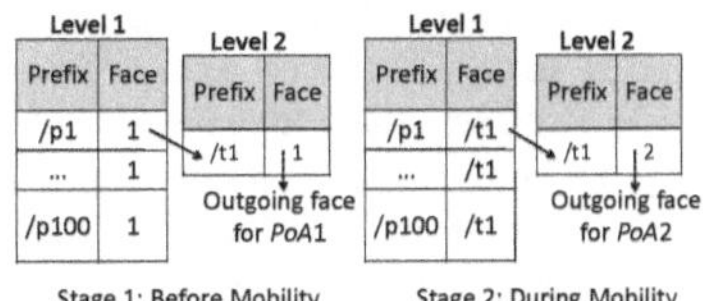

Figure 7.7: **Multi-level FIB in NeMoI.**

by the producer and the name of its *PoA*. The BI can be forwarded to any *MA* located on the shortest path from the producers current location. It should be noted that, non-NeMoI routers can simply forward the BI as an *Interest*. Once a BI reaches a *MA*, it updates its primary/secondary table accordingly. Since the *MAs* maintain a logical one hop connection with each other (overlay network), the receiving *MA* then forwards this BI to the router on the path to its neighbouring *MA*. This routing of BI continues till all the *MAs* are updated with the new location. The *MA* also sends an *Interest* to the producer with a special flag marked to acknowledge the receipt of the mobility update. During forwarding, the NeMoI aware routers update their routing information with the mobility update to widen the scope of propagation. Unlike a dedicated single resolver, in NeMoI the network uses a distributed set of *MAs*. Further, a single prefix is maintained by many *MAs* to ensure robustness and reduce the path inflation.

7.2.3 Multiple logical FIB tables

In NeMoI, we made a design choice to use logically multi-level tables to represent FIB similar to the multi-level forwarding tables used in [138,139]. This choice helps in reducing the number of updates required in the routers, especially when an entire network segment moves. Since the network is organized hierarchically into layers, each level in the FIB can represent the hierarchical layers in the network, with the lower layers pointing to entries in the higher layer tables for lookup *i.e.*, a prefix in a lower layer contains an indirection to a prefix in the next higher layer. *E.g.*, the first level FIB contains prefixes served by the producers and the next *face* to reach the producer at their current *PoA* or the *routable component* located in the next level. The second level in the FIB contains prefixes associated with *PoA* in the network and other prefixes that can be used as the *routable component* by the first level.

Figure 7.6 and 7.7 illustrates the difference between current solutions and the advantage of using multi-level tables like in NeMoI. Let us assume that there are 100 producers associated with their respective prefixes ranging from */p1* to */p100* and these producers are travelling in a train connected to *PoA*1. As shown in Figure 7.6, the FIB entry for these 100 producers would point to *face-1* which is the outgoing *face* for *PoA*1. When the train moves and connects to *PoA*2, all these 100 entries would have to be changed to point to *face-2* which is the outgoing *face* for *PoA*2. In NeMoI, due to logical multi-level tables, only the entry in the "level-2" table is changed from *face-1* to *face-2* as shown in Figure 7.7. This is because the outgoing *face* of the prefix */p1* contains the prefix of the train */t1* as the *routable component*. When the prefix */p1* is looked up in the first level, it leads to an indirection to the level-2 table for the prefix */t1* and the outgoing *face* for */t1* is used for forwarding the *Interest* towards the producer. Therefore, this design choice for multi-level tables effectively reduces the number of updates required in the routers, especially during continuous mobility. Moreover, the producers/consumers within the network-on-the-move need not be informed about the different *PoA*'s they attach to thereby, limiting the signalling traffic and changes to the FIB tables.

The number of tables required is relative to the level of segregation desired in the network and the corresponding implementation strategy involved. Moreover, these are logical tables and can in fact be implemented as one unified table wherein an indirection entry in row 'a' points to another entry in row 'x' in the same table. Similar to [21], we also use a temporary FIB to store the mobility updates in the routers until the control plane synchronizes these update in the data plane of the router. The motivation to use a temporary FIB is similar to that of [21], i.e., only certain nodes with administrative access periodically verify and update the FIBs in the routers in their control. In theory, every change to any of the logical tables in the multi-level table would require a temporary FIB entry. However, in practice, temporary FIBs would exist only for nodes that are continuously moving. For instance, in case of the train scenario, as and when the train changes its *PoA*, it will create a temporary FIB entry for */t1* present in the "level-2" logical table depicted in Figure 7.7. Only when the producer with the prefix */p1* gets out of the train, a temporary FIB entry is created for */p1* in the "level-1" of logical table shown in Figure 7.7.

7.2.4 Synchronization

In NeMoI, the routers on the path from the consumers to producers current location also get updated once an *Interest* flows through that path. However, there still remain the question about updating the old location and the non updated routers on the path to the old location of the mobile producer as shown in Figure 7.8. Therefore, in this section, we describe the two approaches deigned in NeMoI to

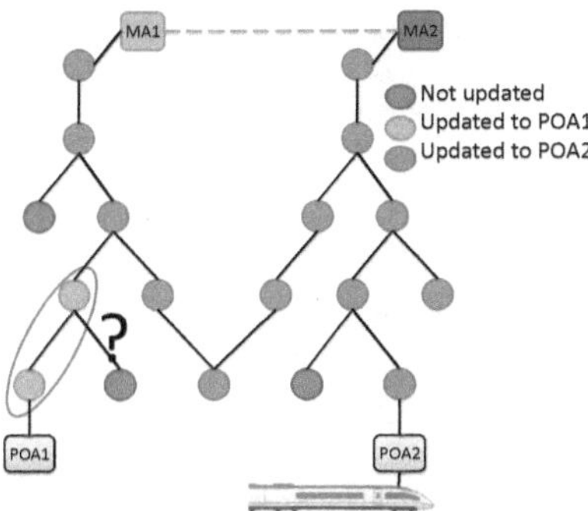

Figure 7.8: **Old location unsynchronized with the mobility update.**

synchronize the old *PoA* and the intermediate NeMoI aware routers on the path to the old *PoA* of the mobile producers with the current mobility update.

7.2.4.1 Proactive version

In the proactive version, when a router receives a BI, it not only forwards the BI to the *MAs* but will also forward it to the old *PoA* of the mobile producer. The first router which forwards the BI towards the old *PoA* sets the *RU* flag to true in the original BI, in order to avoid the downstream routers from sending further updates to the old location. The router makes a copy of the original BI and adds the old *routable component* to the copy. The router then forwards the original BI towards the *MA* and the copied BI to the previous location of the mobile producer using the old *routable component*. As this BI is forwarded towards the old location, all the intermediate NeMoI aware routers on the path to the old location update their routing information. When the BI reaches the old location, the *RU* flag is flipped to false and *RUR* flag is set to true and forwarded towards the router that sent the update as an acknowledgement.

7.2.4.2 Reactive version

In the reactive version, when an *Interest* reaches the old location, the access router at the old location forwards the *Interest* towards the *MA* just like any other router in the network. The *PoA* at the old location also sets an error flag in the *Interest* to notify the *MA* and the routers on the path to *MA* that the producer has moved but mobility update is not yet synchronized in the network. The intermediate NeMoI aware routers update their entries for the prefix and forward the *Interest* towards the *MA*. When a *MA* receives an *Interest* with the error flag, it stores the *Interest* until the mobility update reaches the *MA* or the *Interest* times out. After receiving the BI with the mobility update, the *MA* sets the error flag in the *Interest* to false and adds the new *routable component* to the *Interest* and forwards the *Interest* towards the new location of the producer and thereby reduces the number of packet losses during mobility. In addition to mobility, there are instances when a producer attached to a *PoA* in the network enters in to inactive/sleeping state for some specified duration. In order to not mistaken a sleeping producer for a mobile producer, we recommend the use of technologies like Wake-on-LAN [140], so that the *PoA* can wake up a sleeping producer when an *Interest* is received.

7.2.5 Security

In NeMoI, we inherit the security features of ICN. Similar to RFC 2845 [141], a mobile entity can share the secret keys with the *MAs* for authentication and use one way hash for integrity. However, this implies that intermediate routers cannot update their routing tables. Therefore, in NeMoI, every BI is signed by the endpoint generating the BI *e.g.*, by using the private key of the endpoint. Every intermediate NeMoI aware router and the *MAs* verify the BI using the public key of the endpoint before updating their tables. When the verification is unsuccessful, the BI is dropped to avoid forwarding malicious information and prevent attacks like DOS and FIB pollution. Further, the *MAs* only forward the BI's to their neighbouring *MAs* for synchronizing the mobility updates, they do not modify them. Since the BI is actually signed by the private key of the endpoint, if a rouge *MA* tries to send false BI's or tries to modify and forward the BI, it can be detected during verification. Hence, the availability of *MAs* don't add additional security risk. Further, any security measures designed for controlling *Interest* related attacks (*e.g.*, *Interest* flooding) can be applied to prevent similar attacks using the BI. During synchronization of mobility updates, a *MA* can add its name in the list of *MAs* that are already updated and perform a one way hash of the list for security. This prevents any malicious user/node from modifying the BI and polluting the *MAs* tables. This ensures integrity of the BI and the synchronization can finish elegantly.

7.3 NeMoI: support for mobility scenarios

We explain network mobility in NeMoI using the below scenarios with the example of a train travelling with passengers as network-on-the-move (see Figure 7.1, 7.2 and

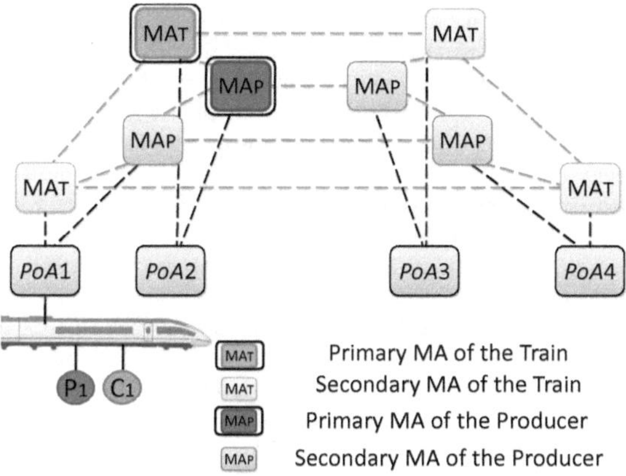

Figure 7.9: **Train mobility.**

Figure 7.9). The passengers in the train can be both consumers and producers. The train itself can also be viewed as a producer associated with a prefix */t1*. When the train starts to move, the consumers and producers in the train are also under mobility. To ensure connectivity, the train, consumer and producer must propagate their mobility information. However, if all the entities under mobility start sending mobility updates for every prefix served by them, the resulting signalling traffic might overwhelm the network. Further, this will result in increasing the number of routing updates. With increased mobility, the signalling traffic might start competing with data traffic for bandwidth.

7.3.1 Producer in network-on-the-move

Let us consider that passengers in the train are producers and they are generating contents via uploading images or video's of their surrounding. In NeMoI, to reduce the signalling traffic, when a producer enters the train and connects to the WiFi access point in the train, the producer sends only a single BI with all the prefixes served by the producer and the prefix of the train */t1* as the *routable component*. This BI is forwarded to the nearest *MA* which in turn updates its neighbours and subsequently the whole network gets updated.

When the train starts moving, it propagates mobility updates by generating a BI at every new *PoA* in the network and the *PoA* forwards the BI to the nearest

MA. Please note that, none of the producers travelling inside the train will send further mobility updates as the train continues to move. During mobility, only the train's mobility update is propagated in the network even though there could be 1000's of producers travelling inside the train each with >=1 prefix. The *MAs* of the train and the intermediate NeMoI aware routers on their path get updated with the current location of the train. Due to our multi-level FIB, the number of updates also reduces as the routers only update the */t1* prefix and not all the prefixes that use it as a *routable component*. For any *Interest* generated for the producers travelling inside the train, the routers will use the *routable component /t1* and forward it to the current location of the producers. Since the train can be used as the *routable component* by other prefixes in the network, if multiple tables are used for representing FIB, then we recommend the prefix */t1* to be located in the second level FIB of the routers to minimize the updates required in the router. The prefixes of the producers travelling in the train can simply point to the prefix of the train in the next higher level in the FIB as shown in Figure 7.7.

In Figure 7.9, the train is travelling from *PoA*1 to *PoA*4. The producer *P1* is a passenger seated in the train. *P1* sends a mobility update with BI containing */p1* as the prefix and */t1* as the *routable component*. This BI reaches the *MAs* of the producer. While the train sends multiple mobility updates one each at *PoA*1, *PoA*2, *PoA*3 and *PoA*4 with BI containing the prefix */t1* and *PoA*x as the *routable component*. This design choice of NeMoI, dramatically reduces the signalling traffic and the number of updates required in the routers. At the same time NeMoI propagates the mobility updates to majority of the routers, reduces the path inflation, packet loss and ensures connectivity. Further, since a single BI can carry all the prefixes served by a producer, it significantly reduces the signalling traffic due to mobility.

7.3.2 Consumer in network-on-the-move

Let us consider that passengers in the train are consumers and they are surfing the Internet to download various contents like news, images, videos, *etc.* When a consumer enters the train, they connect to the train's WiFi access point, hence its *PoA* is */t1*. When the train starts moving, it propagates the mobility updates by generating a BI at every new *PoA* it attaches to. The consumer continues to use the Internet. However, the train network is mobile and the network should be able to route the data towards the current location of the consumer. Since the network is updated with the current location of the train and the consumer is using train's WiFi as the *PoA*, the network simply forwards the data towards the train and the consumer receives it from the train's WiFi.

In Figure 7.9, the train is travelling from *PoA*1 to *PoA*4. The consumer C1 is a passenger in the train. When C1 generates an *Interest*, the *Interest* is forwarded by the train's WiFi access router into the network. In NeMoI, since the train is already propagating the mobility update information and the consumers *PoA* is */t1*, the data is successfully re-routed towards the current location of the consumer in the train. The consumer experiences seamless data transfer while reducing the need for resending *Interest*s for unsatisfied content.

7.3.3 Consumer and producer in network-on-the-move

Let us consider that producer and consumer of a content with the prefix */p1* are travelling in the same train as shown in Figure 7.9. The producer and consumer connect to the WiFi access point in the train and the producer sends a BI with the prefix */p1* and */t1* as the *routable component*. The consumer generates an *Interest* with the prefix */p1* and sends it to the WiFi access router of the train. Since the train's router has already updated its entry for */p1* with the *routable component* as */t1*, the *Interest* is immediately forwarded to the producer in the train. This scenario clearly demonstrates that NeMoI effectively eliminates path inflation.

7.3.4 Nested network-on-the-move

Let us consider a nested network mobility scenario where a passenger travelling the train represents a consumer. The passenger connects his/her mobile phone to the Internet using the WiFi available on the train. Further, the consumer also connects his/her laptop to the WiFi in the mobile phone (via hotspot) to access the Internet forming a nested mobile network.

When the train starts moving, it propagates the mobility update by generating a BI at every *PoA*. When the train is moving, the consumer uses his/her mobile phone and generates an *Interest* to download some content from the Internet. The content is successfully routed back to the consumer using the mobility update generated by the train as discussed in earlier scenarios. When the consumer uses his laptop to access the Internet, the consumer uses the WiFi access point on the mobile phone. The *Interest* is forwarded by the mobile phone to the WiFi access router of the train which in turn forwards it to the network. Upon receiving the content, the WiFi access router in the train will forward it to the WiFi access point of the mobile phone which in turn forwards it to the consumer's laptop. Although the train and consumer's mobile and laptop are in mobility, in NeMoI the consumer's mobile phone and laptop are treated as stationary as the mobility update is taken care by the train.

7.3.5 Travelling from one to another network-on-the-move

Let us consider a passenger in the train as the producer of a content with the prefix
/p1. The producer connects to the WiFi access point in the train and sends a BI
with the prefix */p1* and */t1* as the *routable component*. When the train starts
moving, it propagates the mobility update by generating a BI at every *PoA*. These
BI's are forwarded to the nearest *MA* which in turn updates its neighbours and the
network gets updated. As the train continues to move, the producer does not send
any further mobility updates. The network uses the prefix of the train */t1* as the
routable component to forward any *Interest* to the producer. The producer decides
to change his/her train at a designated stop and enters another train with the prefix
/t2 to continue the jorney. The producer connects to the WiFi access router in the
second train and generates a new BI with the prefix */p1* and *routable component*
/t2 and forwards it to the network. In NeMoI, the old location i.e., the first train
with the prefix */t1* is also notified with this change.

7.3.6 Continuous requests

If a train is moving fast, consumers might not receive the content they request. According to ICN principle, the consumers have to re-initiate the requests, but since
the train is changing its *PoA* so fast, the content might not reach the consumers
in time. Therefore, in NeMoI, we suggest to use proactive caching similar to PeR-
CeIVE [142]. Consumers can include route related information in the *Interest* like
the train's current location, speed, *etc.* Using this information, the data source
can pro-actively cache the data at the respective road side units on the path of the
consumer.

7.4 Chapter summary

In this chapter, we focused on the need for ICN based architectures to support
mobility of the network. We proposed NeMoI, an efficient, robust, reliable and secure
full fledged mobility architecture that is specifically designed to handle network-on-
the-move. NeMoI is designed with distributed *MAs* and logical multi-level FIB tables
to reduce the number of routing updates during mobility. We further optimized
NeMoI to by-pass *MAs* by reactively updating the routers in the path of the request
flow. We also discussed proactive and reactive solutions for synchronizing mobility
updates.

Chapter 8

Application - Network Mobility in Train and Car

In Chapter 7, we proposed *NeMoI* to provide support for network mobility in ICN. NeMoI is a comprehensive solution to support end-points that are within network-on-the-move. These end-points could be producers and/or consumers in network-on-the-move. Moreover, NeMoI is designed to seamlessly support the mobility of consumers and producers who are not located inside a moving network to avoid the need for multiple protocols to support different scenarios. NeMoI encompasses several optimization strategies that make it an efficient solution to support mobility in ICN. In this Chapter, we demonstrate the benefits of NeMoI during deterministic and non-deterministic mobility through journeys in Train and Car. Leveraging the RocketFuel AS1221 topology and a C# simulator we measure the five main network characteristics: signalling traffic, routing updates, effective route optimization, path inflation, and packet loss during network mobility. Evaluations show that NeMoI significantly reduces the amount of signalling traffic, routing updates and path inflation compared to existing solutions while ensuring connectivity for mobile nodes with minimum packet loss for users during mobility. Through various tests, we also establish the effective placement strategy for *MAs* to provide efficient route optimization in NeMoI.

Contents

8.1 Signalling traffic and routing updates

8.1.1 Experimental setup

To demonstrate the effectiveness of NeMoI, we evaluate two types of network mobility patterns: deterministic and non-deterministic. For deterministic network mobility experiment, we introduced network mobility by using the earlier example of a moving train that carried producers and consumers as passengers. To mimic a real train journey, we simulated the famous Australian Indian Pacific train route (the longest train route in Australia) for our evaluation. In the experiment, the train travels from *Perth* to *Sydney* covering a distance of 4,325KM. Whereas for the non-deterministic network mobility experiment, we introduced network mobility with 200 cars, each with a capacity to seat 4 persons. In the experiment, the cars travel from *Perth* to *Sydney*. To make this journey non-deterministic, a random number of cars chose path1 that covers a distance of 3935km while the rest choose path2 which covers 4135km. In order to introduce some more randomness, the cars had several stops along the way.

We assume that at each stop the train and cars have access routers to connect to the Internet and there are numerous Base Stations (BS) between the intermediate cities and stops to provision connection to the Internet. We approximate the coverage area of each BS to 25Miles (40KM) to resemble real world scenario.

For the Dataset, we used the top one Million web site names ranked by the Majestic million website [143] on 04 April 2017. We reversed the website names to resemble hierarchical names in NDN and replaced the '.' in the names with '/'.

For the train and cars along the path1, there were seven stops between *Perth* and *Sydney* while for the cars along the path2, there were eight stops. Accordingly, we

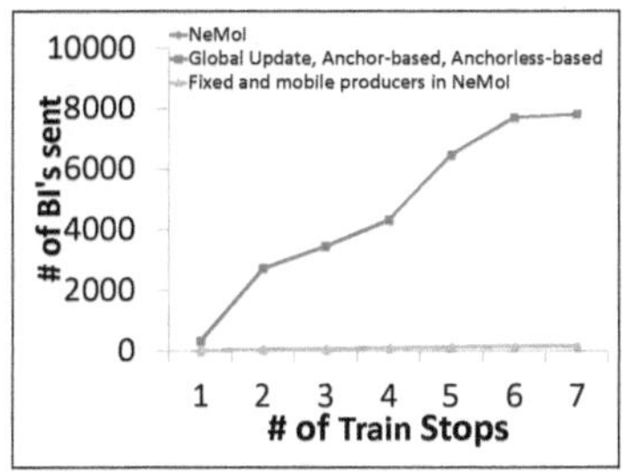

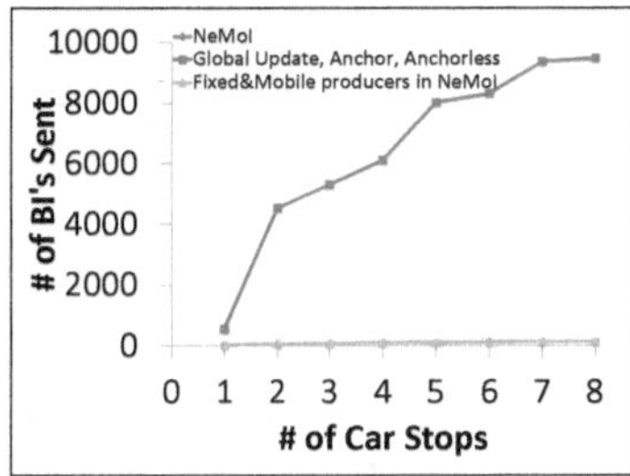

Figure 8.1: **Signalling traffic and routing updates in Train.** Figure 8.2: **Signalling traffic and routing updates in Cars.**

placed seven access routers between the stations/stops in each city for train and path1 and eight access routers for path2. Based on the distance between these cities/stops we introduced 110 BS for the train and 98 BS for path1 and 103 BS for path2 for the cars. To mimic a real mobility scenario and show the impact of mobility, for the train journey, at every stop, 0.16M producers board the train while a random number of producers exit the train. In the car scenario, at each stop in the car's journey 50 passengers enter the cars while random number of passengers exit the cars. This is similar to a Taxi service that picks up and drops off passengers along the journey but the stops and the route taken are not as deterministic as the train. Additionally, we also examined a scenario where a random number of producers were fixed while the rest were mobile. In all of the above mentioned scenarios, during mobility, at every stop and at every BS there is a re-connection to the network.

8.1.2 Deterministic mobility (Train mobility)

We measure the signalling traffic and number of updates in the routing tables incurred due to mobility of the train with three scenarios. In the first scenario, every producer along with the train, produces a BI to notify the network with its mobility update, similar to the global updates, anchor-based and anchor-less solutions [21] (See §2.2.4). In the second scenario, we measure the signalling traffic with NeMoI where the producers notify the network with a mobility update only once when they board the train. In the third scenario, we introduce a mixed set of fixed and mobile producers in NeMoI. The number of BI's generated in these scenarios are equivalent to the number of routing updates. The train continues to notify the network at every point where it re-connects. When the train re-connects to the network through a *PoA*, the *PoA* sends the BI to any *MA* on the shortest path and the *MAs* route this update among themselves.

We observe from the results in Figure 8.1 that NeMoI generated ~4.6M mobility updates in scenario 2 and ~3.7M mobility updates in scenario 3. Whereas other standard solutions like global updates, anchor-based, anchor-less based solutions and without the logical multi-level FIB optimization in NeMoI ~0.215B mobility updates were generated. The results show that with NeMoI, there is a dramatic decrease in the signalling traffic and the routing updates compared to the existing solutions. We also observe that, NeMoI ensures reachability and faster updates compared to global updates. It should be noted that in these results, we assigned only a single prefix to each producer. If the producers serve more than one prefix and generated a mobility update for every prefix then signalling traffic and routing updates would be even higher.

8.1.3 Non-deterministic Mobility (Car mobility)

In this experiment, we measure the signalling traffic and number of updates in the routing tables incurred due to mobility of the 200 cars with a random number of cars travelling on path1 and the rest travelling on path2 with three scenarios. We treat all passengers and drivers in the cars as producers in this experiment. In the first scenario, every producer along with the cars, produce a BI to notify the network with their mobility update. This behaviour is similar to the current state of the art global updates, anchor-based and anchor-less solutions [21] (See §2.2.4). In the second scenario, we measure the signalling traffic with NeMoI where the producers notify the network with a mobility update only once when they enter the car. In the third scenario, we introduce a mixed set of fixed and mobile producers in NeMoI. Similar to the train scenario, the number of BI's generated in these scenarios are equivalent to the number of routing updates. The cars continue to notify the network at every point in the network where it re-connects to the network. When a car re-connects to the network through a *PoA*, the *PoA* sends the BI to any MA on the shortest path and the MA's will synchronize this update among themselves.

We observe from the results in Figure 8.2 that NeMoI generated 3,767 mobility updates in scenario 2 and 3,245 mobility updates in scenario 3. Whereas other state of the art solutions like global updates, anchor-based, anchor-less based solutions and without the logical multi-level FIB optimization in NeMoI 243,340 mobility updates were generated. Similar to the train scenario, we see from the results that with NeMoI there is a significant decrease in the signalling traffic and routing updates compared to the existing solutions. We also observe that, NeMoI ensures reachability and faster updates compared to global updates. Similar to the train scenario, we assigned only a single prefix to each producer in these experiments. Since producers use a single BI packet for all of their prefixes (deterministic or non-deterministic),

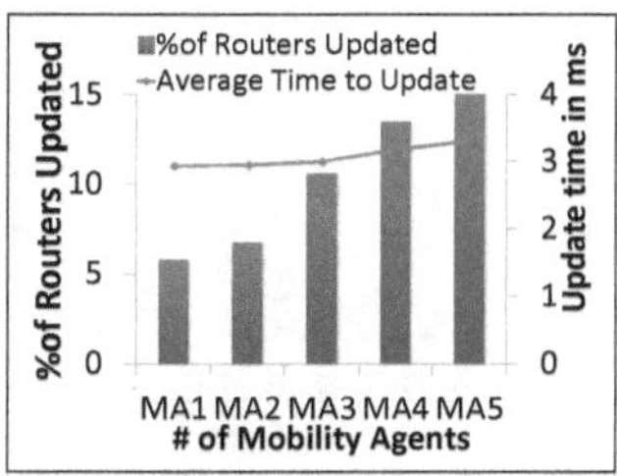

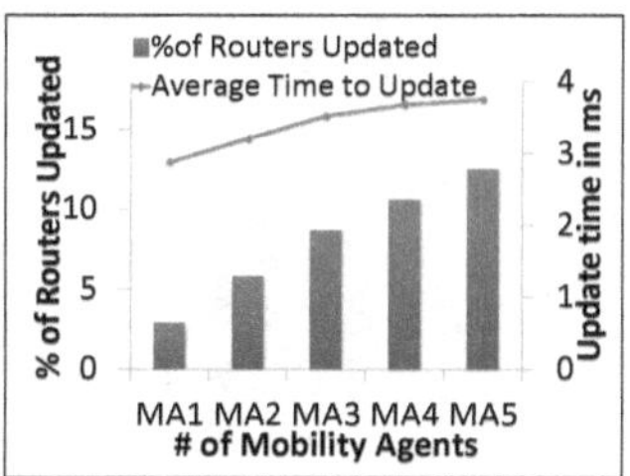

Figure 8.3: **Mobility updates with Core MA placement strategy.** Figure 8.4: **Mobility updates with Edge MA placement strategy.**

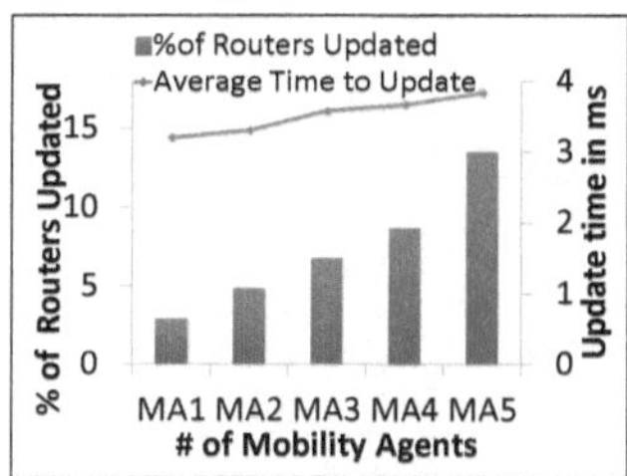

Figure 8.5: **Mobility updates with Random MA placement strategy.**

the number of packets is reduced to 1 for each producer in comparison to a design where each prefix has to be carried in a separate BI (i.e., no. of prefixes = no. of BI's).

8.2 Effective route optimization

We realized that with NeMoI, the effective placement of *MAs* is a key to achieve effective route optimization and to gain maximum performance benefit. So we used the network mobility with train as an example to evaluate the effect of *MA* placements, we choose three different placement strategies namely: Core, Edge and Random for placing the *MAs* respectively at the core, edge and random locations in the Rocket-Fuel AS1221 topology. Placing the *MAs* at the edge of the network could result in reduced path inflation. However, it can affect the propagation of mobility updates and in turn contribute to increasing the overall path inflation. Placing the *MAs* at the core of the network seems to provide more promising results as it can increase

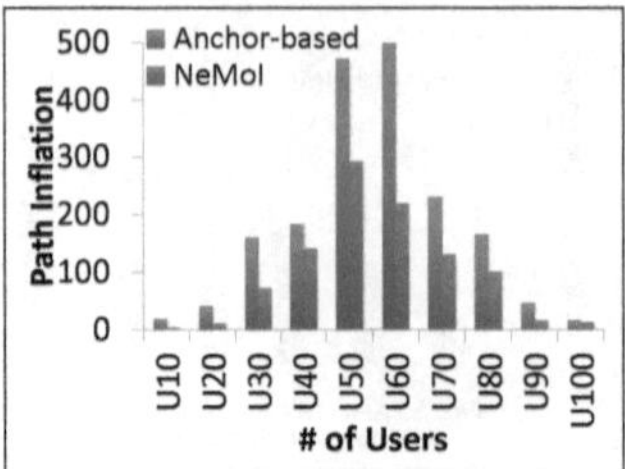
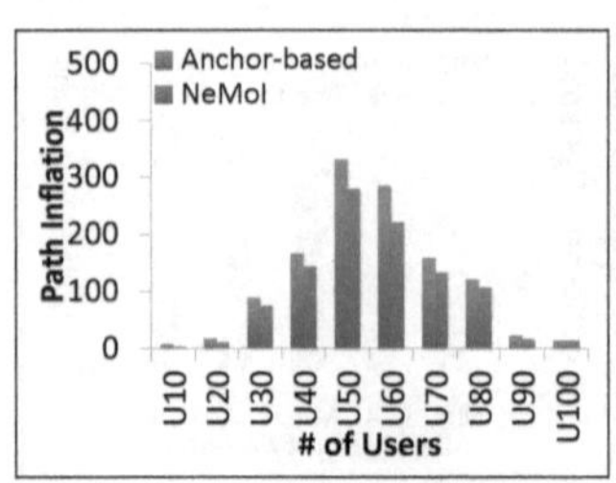

Figure 8.6: **Path inflation in Anchor and NeMoI with Core placement strategy.**

Figure 8.7: **Path inflation in Anchor and NeMoI with Edge placement strategy.**

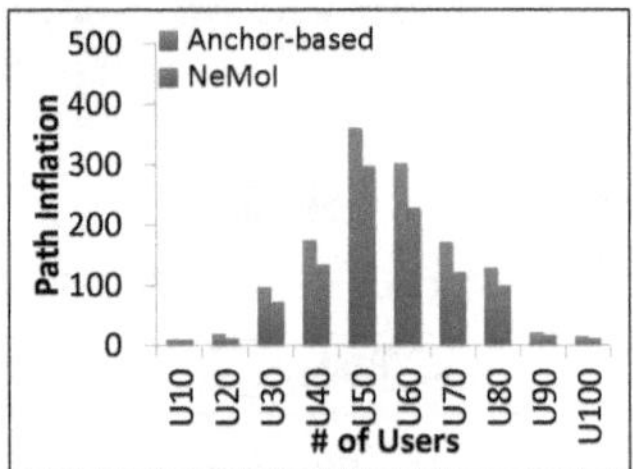

Figure 8.8: **Path inflation in Anchor and NeMoI with Random placement strategy.**

the propagation of mobility updates. However, there is also a possibility that the placement of *MAs* might not be a significant factor so, even a random placement of *MAs* would be sufficient.

Hence, we investigated the behaviour of NeMoI with all three placement strategies and with different number of *MAs*. We begin with one *MA* and gradually increased the number of *MAs* to five. We placed a single producer in *Adelaide*. The producer generated a BI after attaching to the router1737 in *Adelaide*. Further, we also measured for each placement, the percentage of intermediate routers that were updated and the time to update them. We observe from the results in Figure 8.3, 8.4 and 8.5 that Core *MA* placement performs the best out of the three choices and updates maximum number of routers in the network with the least amount of time. We also observed that the percentage of routers updated increased with increase in the number of *MAs*.

8.3 Path inflation

Path inflation is an unavoidable consequence of indirection. In NeMoI, since *Interests* are redirected towards *MAs* for resolution, a concern emerges for path inflation experienced by the consumers. The design choices in NeMoI try to minimize path inflation if not eliminate it entirely. It is a trade-off we believe that has to be made to ensure connectivity and reachability with mobility. Since we use *MAs* similar to anchor-based solutions, we compare the path inflation in NeMoI with that of anchor-based solutions.

8.3.1 Experimental setup

For this experiment, we placed a producer in *Adelaide* and associated 101 consumers, one each to every router in the topology (1:1). The consumer arrival process followed a normal distribution.

8.3.2 Experiment

First, we measured the path inflation experienced by consumers in NeMoI and compared it to anchor-based solutions by leveraging the three different *MA* placement strategies described earlier with five *MAs*. The consumers arrived and generated *Interests* accordingly. We then measured path inflation by counting the number of hops the *Interest* traveled to reach the producer. For this experiment, in NeMoI, when the producer sent a BI, the *MAs* and the intermediate routers that forward the BI were updated. We observe from the results in Figure 8.6, 8.7 and 8.8 that path inflation in NeMoI is considerably lower compared to anchor-based solutions. Further, consumers experienced the lowest path inflation with Core *MA* placement.

Second, we measured the path inflation in NeMoI using two different scenarios. In the first scenario, we measured cumulative path inflation by counting the number of hops the *Interest* traveled when the producer sent a BI and only *MAs* were updated. In the second scenario, we measured the same, but along with *MAs* the intermediate routers that forward the BI were also updated.

We observe from the results in Figure 8.9, 8.10 and 8.11 that NeMoI reduces path inflation by allowing the intermediate routers to update their routing information when they forward BI to the *MAs*. Again we observe that Core *MA* placement strategy outperforms Edge and Random placements. Further, NeMoI also allows

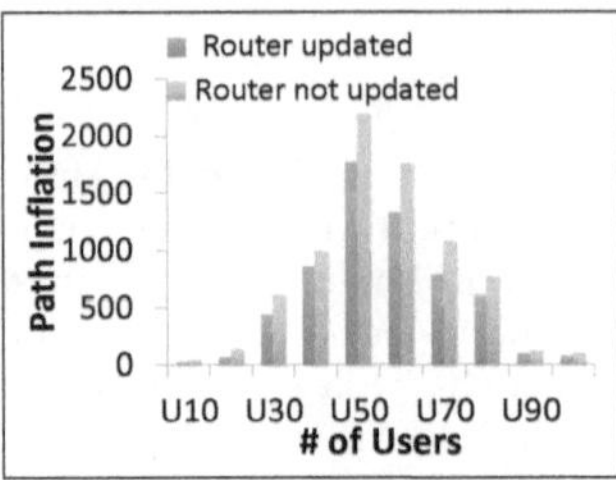

Figure 8.9: **Comparison of path inflation in NeMoI with/without router updates (Core).**

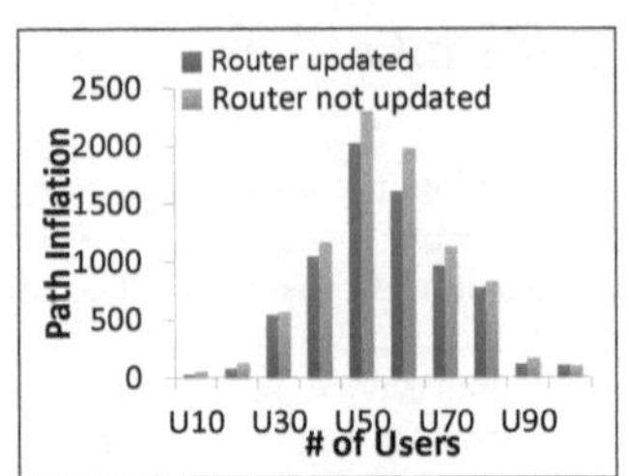

Figure 8.10: **Comparison of path inflation in NeMoI with/without router updates (Edge).**

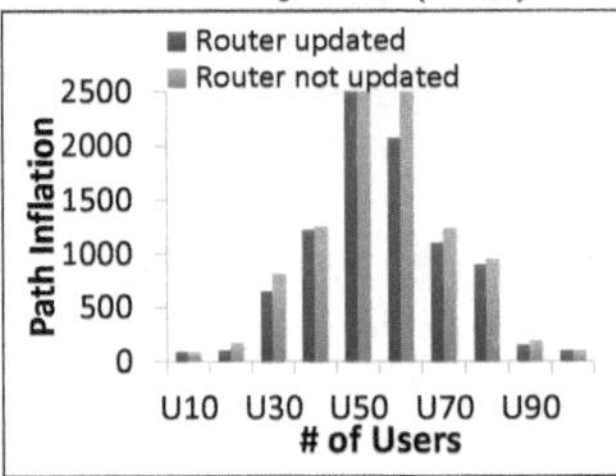

Figure 8.11: **Comparison of path inflation in NeMoI with/without router updates (Random).**

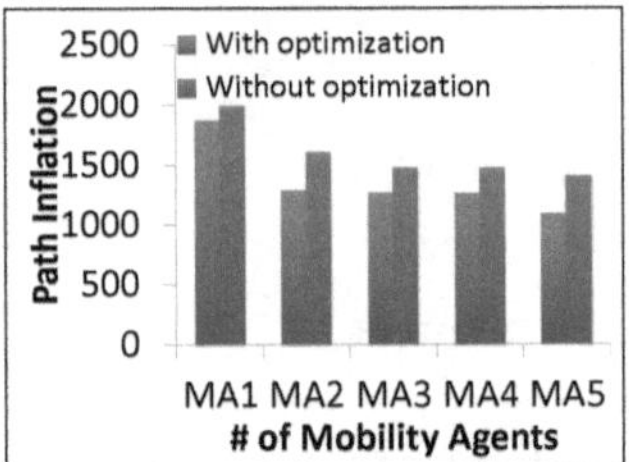

Figure 8.12: **Path inflation with increasing MA in NeMoI during network mobility.**

rest of the network to gradually update reactively as they forward *Interest* towards the producer via the *MAs*.

Third, we analyzed the effect of increasing the number of *MAs* in NeMoI. We measured the cumulative path inflation in the Core placement strategy with two scenarios. In the first scenario, whenever the producer sent a BI, the intermediate routers were allowed to update their routing tables while in the second scenario the intermediate routers were not allowed to update their routing tables. For the same consumer arrival process described earlier, we increased the number of *MAs* from 1 to 5 and measured the cumulative path inflation for the consumers. We observe from the results in Figure 8.12 that as we increased the number of *MAs*, the path inflation started to decrease. Further, we observe that path inflation reduced when the intermediate routers were allowed to update their routing information. Therefore, with the right number of *MAs*, we can significantly minimize the path inflation in NeMoI.

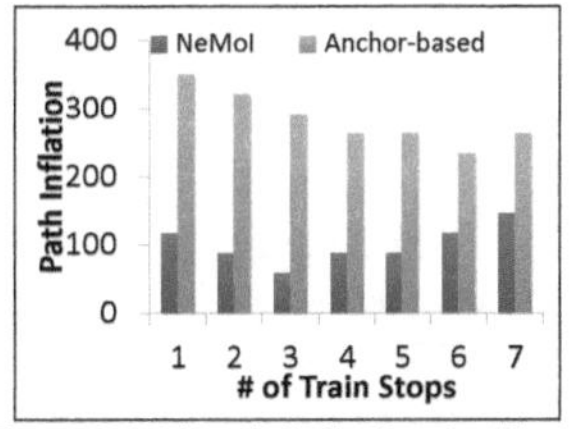

Figure 8.13: **Path inflation in Train.**

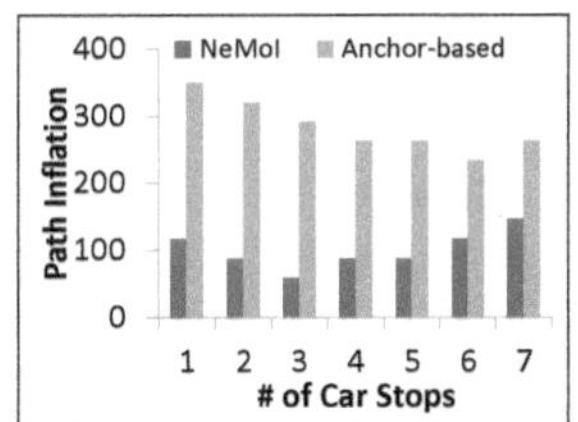

Figure 8.14: **Path inflation in Car.**

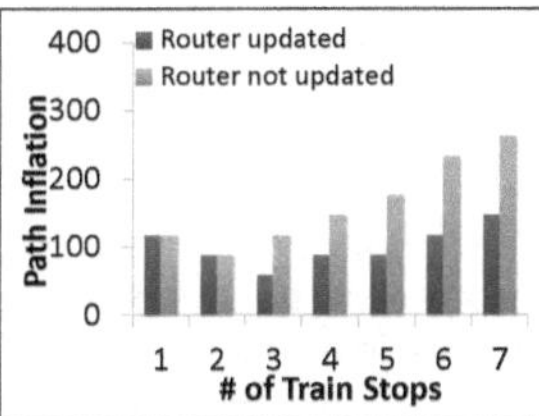

Figure 8.15: **Path inflation with optimization in NeMoI during network mobility.**

Last, we measure the path inflation experienced by consumers travelling in the train and the cars. At each stop, consumers travelling in the train and cars generated an *Interest* for the content produced by an immobile producer located in *Adelaide*. In the first scenario, we measured the cumulative path inflation experienced by the consumer in NeMoI and compared it with anchor-based solutions. In the second scenario, we measured the cumulative path inflation experienced by the consumer in NeMoI when the intermediate routers were allowed to update their routing information with the mobility update and compared it to the case when the routers were not allowed to update.

We observe from the results in Figure 8.13 and Figure 8.14 that total path inflation experienced by consumers in NeMoI is only 24 hops, compared to 68 hops in anchor-based solutions. Further, Figure 8.15 also shows that path inflation decreases considerably when intermediate routers are also updated.

8.4 Packet loss

Since the producers in the train and cars are constantly moving during their journey from *Perth* to *Sydney* they are re-connecting to the Internet at every access router and BS in the network. As a result during every re-connection the train and cars send a mobility update (BI) to the network to propagate the information of their current *PoA*. However, there is an unavoidable synchronization delay involved until the information is propagated to all the nodes in the network. During this time, if any user sends an Interest for the data served by the train, cars or any producer travelling in these moving network, the Interest cannot be satisfied if there were no cached copies. This is a direct consequence of mobility, which is aggravated with the increasing number of mobility update as the network is unstable. Hence we measured the amount of packet loss in NeMoI during mobility.

8.4.1 Experimental setup

During the journey from *Perth* to *Sydney* the train is reconnecting at 110 BS, similarly, the cars travelling in path1 reconnects at 98 BS while those on path2 reconnects at 103 BS and send BI during each reconnection. We configured the simulator to assume the delay of 1ms for propagating the mobility information to the nearest *MA*. We used five routers as *MAs* and assigned 101 consumers to each remaining router in the network.

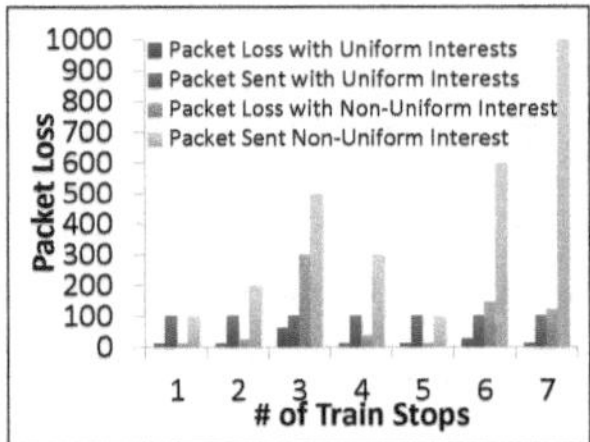

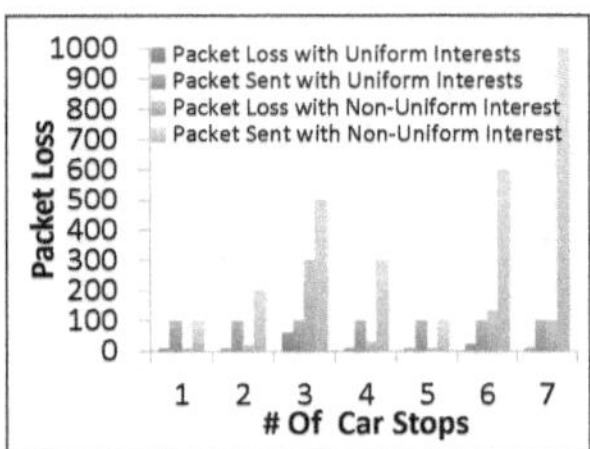

Figure 8.16: **Packet loss in Train in NeMoI during network mobility.**

Figure 8.17: **Packet loss in Car in NeMoI during network mobility.**

8.4.2 Experiment

For the deterministic and non-deterministic scenarios, the train/cars started their journey from *Perth* to *Sydney*. The 101 consumers generated Interests according to a normal distribution and non-uniform arrival pattern. In the non-mobility case all the Interests would be satisfied by the network. However since during the mobility update the network is unstable, as a consequence, some Interests will be dropped and this results in packet loss. The packet loss at the onset of mobility update propagation is inevitable unless the Data was already cached in some routers. For this experiment, we turned off caching to measure the amount of packet loss during mobility. The results are shown in Figure 8.16 and 8.17. We observed from the results that NeMoI tried to minimize packet loss with faster propagation of mobility update. Please note that at stop 3 users experienced maximum packet loss because there were 48 reconnections (BS) between stop2 and stop3 compared to other stops where reconnections ranged between 8 to 22.

Through these evaluations we demonstrate the effects of mobility in the network. We evaluated NeMoI with standard state-of-the-art solutions and showed that NeMoI significantly reduced the signalling traffic and path inflation. We also evaluated effective route optimizations with three placement strategies for *MA* and showed that Core placement provides maximum benefits. In NeMoI, there is no need for a MA in every users Home Network like in Mobile IP, but the *MAs* is an additional function of the nodes in the network. With just 5 *MAs* we showed a reduction in the number of network updates and increase in the propagation of mobility updates. With a careful design of the *MA* service it is possible to choose the suitable number of *MAs* to achieve the desired performance. Intuitively, it can be seen that since NeMoI greatly reduces the signalling traffic w.r.to the state-of-the-art solutions, the energy consumption in NeMoI is proportional to the signalling traffic. We observe from the evaluations that NeMoI reduced the total traffic from 0.215B to 4.6M and total number of hops from 68 to 24. Such reduction also has energy related benefits [144].

8.5 Chapter summary

In this chapter we evaluated the performance of NeMoI, the architecture for network mobility in ICN proposed in Chapter 7. Leveraging a real world topology with one million dataset we showed that NeMoI performs 47times better than global updates and other existing solutions. The results show that NeMoI dramatically reduced the signalling traffic, routing updates, path inflation and minimized packet loss in both deterministic and non-deterministic mobility scenarios. We also examined three important placement strategies for *MAs* and established an effective placement strategy to provide efficient route optimization.

Chapter 9

EVA: A Distributed Optimization Architecture for Efficient Video Analysis

Deep Neural Networks (DNN) are popularly used to improve the prediction accuracy of video analysis. However, DNNs are computationally expensive as they demand higher resources. Moreover, video analysis applications require low latency, high bandwidth and storage. Hence, video traffic is increasingly pushed to the Edge to improve network performance and reduce the load on the Cloud. This chapter tackles the resource-accuracy optimization issues associated with DNN applications through a distributed architecture named EVA and understands the video analysis application's requirements. We noticed that timeliness of anomaly detection is crucial in many video analysis applications along with minimal resource utilization. Therefore, this chapter studies the overhead of profiling techniques which are commonly used to find optimal DNN configurations during video analysis to achieve good resource-accuracy trade-offs. To minimize this overhead, we propose the 2-stage deep learning approach which eliminates the need for profiling by building efficient and robust DNNs and produces better resource-accuracy trade-offs. We further propose two rate adaption algorithms: Adaptive Frame Rate (AFR) and Adaptive Resolutions (ARR) to optimize the video analysis and resource consumption, bandwidth and storage during video analysis with DNN.

The key contributions in this work include:

- A distributed optimization architecture called EVA for efficient video analysis using DNNs.
- 2-stage deep learning to build robust DNNs with high accuracy for eliminating profiling.

- Adaptive Rate algorithms: AFR and ARR to optimize the performance of video analysis.
- Reduce the bandwidth and storage consumption.

Contents

9.1 EVA overview

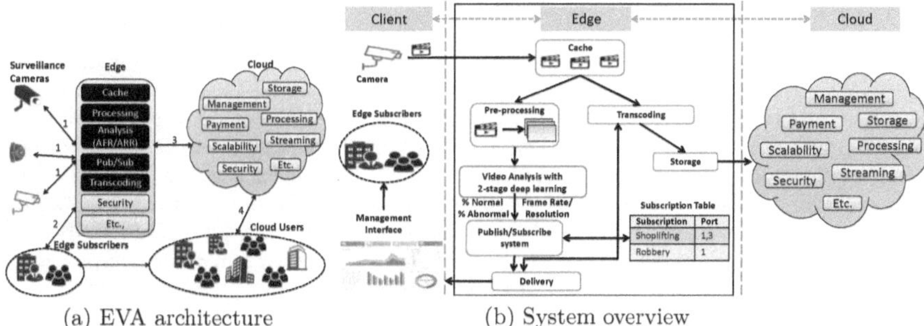

      (a) EVA architecture   (b) System overview

Figure 9.1: **EVA design and system overview.**

9.1.1 EVA architecture

The proposed distributed architecture of EVA is shown in Figure 9.1 (a) while a detailed functional overview of a system implementing the services is shown in Figure 9.1 (b). Through literature survey, we identified the minimal set of services in

EVA for efficiently supporting the requirements of Video surveillance and Management System (VMS) applications. Essentially, we provide the services for caching, coding, video analysis and pub/sub at the Edge while utilizing the long-term storage and streaming services of the Cloud. We choose the caching and coding services at the Edge since studies in [52] have shown that caching has the potential to increase revenue for the service provider. Further, many VMS applications require timely delivery of event notification and mostly rely on human support for constant monitoring. Therefore, we provide video analysis and pub/sub services at the Edge to eliminate such temporal dependency and deliver the notifications in time when an event of interest occurs, and thereby minimize the need for human monitoring. With the help of these services, we aim to steer the surveillance video traffic towards Edge [53–56], and alleviate it from consuming bandwidth in the core network and further fulfill the low latency requirement of many video analysis applications.

Through the management interface in EVA, the Edge service provider advertises the services for video analysis, processing, transcoding, pub/sub, storage, *etc.* The customers can opt for any/all of these services. The pricing and Service Level Agreement (SLA) for the services offered at the Edge is out of scope of this chapter, however, they can be provided on the management interface. For security, we assume that standard requirements will be met by the Edge service provider. For further readings about security at Edge we refer the readers to recent works [145–147]. Once an agreement is concurred between the customer and the Edge service provider, the applications can start using the services shown in Figure 9.1. Essentially, the surveillance cameras start to monitor their surroundings and simultaneously upload their videos to the Edge for analysis. Since the Edge is located close to the user, the latency to upload the video is dramatically reduced, and the video traffic in the core network is also avoided. Edge provides the 2-stage deep learning (see §9.2) video analysis algorithms to detect interested anomalies in the uploaded videos. Once the video is uploaded, it is stored in the cache temporarily for a duration selected by the client at the time of buying the service. The video is then sent to the pre-processing module which splits it into individual frames. These frames are then fed into the DNNs for detecting anomalies.

During analysis we use one of the two adaptive rate algorithms: AFR or ARR (see §9.4) based on the application and Edge's requirements to optimize the performance of video analysis, bandwidth and storage. Even though, EVA is capable of detecting many different abnormal activities during video analysis, in this chapter for simplicity, we analyze the surveillance videos to detect normal and abnormal behaviours such as shoplifting, car accidents, robbery, *etc.*, provided in the UCF-Crime dataset [61]. The result from the video analysis process will contain the class of the video from the UCF-Crime dataset *e.g.*, Normal, Shoplifting, Car accidents, *etc.* The video analysis also outputs the percentage of normal and abnormal activity found in the video alon with the frame rate and resolution used to analyze the respective video. The results are then forwarded to the pub/sub module.

In order to avoid re-inventing the wheel, we refer to existing pub/sub architectures in IP and future Internet architectures such as ICN [6] and COPSS [3] to offer a controlled and efficient pub/sub service. In this work, we leverage COPSS as the exemplary pub/sub architecture. The pub/sub module maintains a subscription table with the list of anomalies such as Shoplifting and Robbery that subscribers are interested in along with the outgoing ports that publisher should use to send the notification messages to the subscribers. The consumers (authorities, security agents, *etc.*) interested in receiving notifications upon detecting anomalies subscribe to this service via the management interface. We use a pub/sub model specifically to avoid the temporal dependency between the subscriber and publisher for the abnormal events. Since it is not known when an abnormal activity takes place, the pub/sub model is a good candidate to send event notifications to the subscribers in time when an activity of interest is detected. Additionally, we use the pub/sub module to send feedback information from video analysis to the subscribers to dictate the frame rate or resolution for uploading the videos to the Edge for optimizing the bandwidth utilization.

Transcoding is a standard operation used to generate videos with different bit rates (quality) for streaming the videos to viewers with different available download bandwidth [148, 149]. Parallel to video analysis, the transcoding module codes the videos in the cache to different bitrates as per the QoS indicated by the producer. For the surveillance videos, after the video analysis, the frame rate and the resolution used to analyze the video is forwarded to the transcoding module via the delivery module. The transcoding module uses this feedback and directs the storage module to store the video in the Cloud at this frame rate and resolution. The storage module opportunistically stores the video in the Cloud whenever the bandwidth is available. The video is stored in the Cloud for long-term storage and streaming.

9.1.2 Video analysis in EVA

During video analysis, the video is classified in to Normal or Abnormal class based on its content. The resulting classification, prediction accuracy, frame rate and resolution of every video is forwarded to the pub/sub module. The resulting frame rate and resolution is also forwarded to the storage module. Upon detecting anomalies during video analysis such as when a video is classified as Abnormal, the video analysis module also sends an event notification request to the pub/sub module with the video details (*e.g.*, ID or name) and the obtained classification and prediction accuracy. Once the publisher in the pub/sub module receives this request, it generates an event notification with a publication packet containing the video ID and the observed abnormal behaviour (*e.g.*, Shoplifting) and looks up the subscription table to obtain the ports to forward the packet. The publication packet is forwarded to the delivery module. The delivery module forwards the publication packet to the respective outgoing port(s) and sends a wait packet with the duration set by the application (*e.g.*, 24hrs) to the Transcoding module with the details of the video to retain it in the cache as it is most likely to be requested by the subscribers for inspection. A trade off here is to retain multiple copies in caches at the Edge and at the Cloud, however, Pang *et al.* [52] show that caching at the Edge has the potential to increase payoff for service providers. The delivered notification appears on the management interface, and the subscriber can request to download the video for inspection using standard streaming protocols offered by the Edge (*e.g.*, DASH [150]) that is embedded in the management interface. Subsequently, the video is delivered to the subscribers via the delivery module. The resulting frame rate/resolution for the next video segments is sent as a feedback from the pub/sub module to the subscribers to control the video upload to the Edge in order to efficiently utilize the bandwidth. Optionally, when normal activity is detected, the publisher in the pub/sub module can send a periodic update notification to the subscribers with a status OK message using the same publication packet. Simultaneously, the frame rate/resolution that were used during the video analysis are forwarded to the storage module, which uses this feedback to store the videos in the Cloud with the frame rates and resolution used during video analysis. The underlying principle is to store the videos with normal content at lower frame rates and lower resolutions while videos with anomalous content are stored at higher frame rates and higher resolutions and, thereby reduce the overall storage requirement.

9.2 2-stage deep learning

Video analysis is the core component of surveillance applications. During analysis, there is always a trade-off between *resource demand* and *prediction accuracy*. In other words, highly accurate DNNs consume higher resources [14]. For instance, DNNs need about 30 Gflops to process a single frame when detecting an object [28]. Hence, most video analysis approaches use profiling to find optimal configurations [14, 32] to achieve better resource-accuracy trade off.

Profiling is usually performed either at the start of the analysis or periodically at regular intervals, and studies show that periodic re-profiling delivers an improved performance [14, 32]. However, profiling is an expensive operation and adds additional overhead during video analysis [32]. Zhang *et al.* [32] show that profiling needs specialized hardware such as GPU's along with parallelization and sampling to speed up the process of selecting optimal configurations for video analysis. Usually, the Edge delivers low latency requirements demanded by many applications such as VMS and hence, the overhead of profiling may hinder fulfilling this requirement. Further, video also consumes a lot of bandwidth along with storage which is an expensive component of the video analysis applications [58–60].

In order to eliminate the need for profiling in video analysis, we propose a 2-stage deep learning approach to build efficient and robust DNNs in the respective *offline* and *online* stages. Essentially, during the offline stage we build efficient DNNs by exploiting the vast amount of already existing video data from the video analysis applications. It is well known that, performance of any machine learning model including deep learning with DNNs is highly dependent on the type and amount of available training data. Therefore, it is important to train the DNNs with all possible scenarios that it is expected to identify when it is deployed in the real world. However, newer scenarios such as threats/crimes during video surveillance are introduced constantly and it is difficult to capture all possible scenarios during training. Therefore, in EVA, we propose to train the DNNs initially with available data in the offline stage and continue training the DNNs with newer incoming video data on the fly in the online stage in parallel to video analysis. Thus, we build robust DNNs, that improve the performance and overall accuracy of detection.

In EVA, we want to optimize the complex operation of classifying the videos into their respective categories (Normal, Shoplifting, *etc.*) during analysis to improve the accuracy of detecting incidents; rather than simple object detection which has lower accuracy and does not consider temporal information which exists between frames in the video. Many traditional video analysis applications that perform object detection utilize CNNs. However, standard CNNs can only extract spatial features from static images. Extensions such as from Karpathy *et al.* [151] which extend the standard CNNs to extract temporal features from the videos produce lower accuracies with increased complexity. Moreover, Karpathy *et al.* also mention that RNNs are more powerful than CNNs and they wish to explore RNNs in the future. Hence, we realized that CNNs are not enough and we explored the combination of transfer learning, CNN, and RNN to build robust and highly accurate DNNs. Essentially, we utilize the Google's InceptionV3 CNN network that was pre-trained using the Imagenet's dataset. We leverage this CNN and transfer learning with the UCF-Crime dataset to build efficient RNNs. The RNNs are built using the Long Short Term Memory (LSTM) architecture as it can maintain the temporal relationship between the frames in a video and significantly improve the accuracy of detection.

In this chapter, we leverage the UCF-Crime dataset along with its ground truth to build the RNNs for video analysis. We divide the UCF-Crime dataset into 3 categories: training, validation and online dataset. We build the DNNs with commercially used [152, 153] frame rates (6fps, 8fps, 10fps, 15fps and 30fps) and resolutions (240p, 480p, 720p).

As, the required depth *i.e.*, the layers in any DNN is not known a priori, similar to Sahoo *et al.* [50], we begin by building a shallow DNN during offline stage with just one layer and one video segment. We then validate the performance of the DNN with the ground truth from the UCF-Crime dataset using the videos in the validation dataset. Subsequently, we increase the layers of the DNNs to 12, 16, 20, 30, 128 and so on when we observe a degradation in the resulting F1 score (prediction accuracy) of the DNN [50]. F1 score is the harmonic mean between precision and recall and it is commonly used in machine learning to determine the outputs of analysis. The F1 score usually lies between 0 and 1, where 0 represents the lowest and 1 represents the highest measured qualities. Please note that except the DNN layers, frame rate and resolution, we fixed the remaining DNN configuration knobs such as loss, optimizer, regularizer, activation, *etc.*, during the training. We continue the offline training process until we build accurate and deep enough DNNs (*e.g.*, 1024 layers) that can efficiently analyze the videos and produce results with higher accuracies. We repeat this process for building a DNN for each selected frame rate and resolution. The DNN is then trained with all the remaining offline training videos in the dataset. During the offline training, every DNN is assigned a benchmark threshold value for the normal content that it can detect based on the data used to train the DNN. We noticed that every DNN (for each selected frame rate and resolution) had a separate threshold value based on its accuracy of prediction. This is due to the possible and yet, acceptable degradation in the prediction accuracy of the DNNs with lesser frames and resolutions as they have less data points to learn.

In the online stage, we continue to use the DNNs built in the offline stage, to predict newer incoming videos. Additionally, we re-train the DNNs in parallel with the new incoming videos. We continue to use these DNNs until a degradation in the accuracy below an established threshold (*e.g.*, 75%) is detected for any of the DNNs. The threshold is an application specific tunable parameter and is subject to the type of videos under analysis. Once a degradation is detected, we re-train that DNN's configurations by increasing the number of its DNN layers to improve its prediction accuracy/F1 score. Since we use F1 score as a metric to improve the performance of the DNNs we can avoid the need for periodic re-profiling during video analysis. Instead, in EVA, we use the prediction accuracy of each video segment to find the DNNs with the best configurations for analyzing the next video segment and thereby, eliminate the overhead of profiling.

Table 9.1: **System environment.**

Environment	Parameter	Description
Current environment	x_t	% of normal content in v_t
	p_t	Threshold for normal content at t
	l_t	Length of v_t
	r_t	Frame rate selected for v_t
	ρ_t	Resolutions selected for v_t
	M_t	RNN selected for v_t
Next video segment	l_{t+1}	Length of v_{t+1}
	F_{t+1}	Original Frame count in v_{t+1}
	R_{t+1}	Original Resolution of v_{t+1}
	$\vec{n}$	M available DNNs for v
Adaptive Rate Decision	r_{t+1}	Frame rate selected for v_{t+1}
	ρ_{t+1}	Resolution selected for v_{t+1}
	M_{t+1}	DNN for v_{t+1}
	p_{t+1}	Threshold for normal content

Algorithm 1: AdaptiveRate

---

1 **Function** AdaptiveRate(S_{v_t},AFR,ARR,$c1$,$c2$):
2   **if** AFR **then**
3 | Function AFR (S_{v_t},$c1$,$c2$)
4   **else**
5 | Function ARR (S_{v_t},$c1$,$c2$)
6   **end**
7   return $S_{v_{t+1}}$
8 **return**

9.3 System model

We studied that *frame rate* and *resolution* are the most dominant video metrics [14, 31] during analysis. The idea behind our approach to optimize video analysis is to build robust DNNs that eliminate profiling by utilizing *rate adaption* with different frame rates and resolutions. The motivation for rate adaption is the insight that, most of the videos captured during surveillance tend to have normal content and suspicious/abnormal activities such as robbery, shoplifting, car accidents, *etc.*, are infrequent and occur for a very short duration [51]. However, the timely detection of these abnormal events with high accuracy is a crucial requirement [51] of surveillance applications.

In the next section, we propose two rate adaptive algorithms for optimizing the video analysis process. As the prerequisite, in this section, we extract the corresponding system environment required by the rate adaptive algorithms in EVA. In a video analysis environment, let v_t be the current video segment (chunk), where a segment refers to a small portion of the entire video stream, $e.g.$, 2min segments of a 2hr long video stream. Let ℓ_t, F_t and R_t be the length (video duration), frame count and resolution of the video segment v_t respectively. Let x_t be the percentage of normal content present in the video v_t based on the ground truth from the existing videos/golden configuration [31]. Golden configurations are generally used in the absence of ground truth to validate the output of machine learning algorithms. They are usually expensive as they demand high resources and use the best configurations but, they are known to produce highest accuracies and hence desired for cross-validation. In our prediction model, p_t is the benchmarked normal video threshold value of the DNN selected for v_t, wherein each DNN has a separate threshold. The threshold is based on the observed normal content during the offline testing. Similarly, r_t and ρ_t are the frame rate and resolutions of v_t respectively. Finally, M_t is the DNN selected for analyzing v_t and $\overrightarrow{n}_t$ is the number of available DNNs for rate adaption. The complete system environment for rate adaptive algorithms is listed in Table 9.1. During analysis, after the prediction of every video segment v_t, the following state information $S_{v_{t+1}}$ is collected.

$$S_{v_{t+1}} = \left[x_t, p_t, r_t, \rho_t, \ell_{t+1}, R_{t+1}, F_{t+1}, r_{t+1}, \rho_{t+1}, p_{t+1}, M_{t+1}, \overrightarrow{n}_{t+1} \right].$$

9.4 EVA algorithms

A pseudocode of the AdaptiveRate algorithm in EVA is shown in algorithm1. Given the state S_{v_t} with the current system environment, and the selection between AFR or ARR, the algorithm will select an optimal DNN for the next video segment v_{t+1} such that,

$$\pi : \pi \left(S_{v_{t+1}}, M_{t+1} \right) \to [0,1] \, ,$$

where $\pi \left(S_{v_{t+1}}, M_{t+1} \right)$ is the probability that a DNN M_{t+1} is chosen for the state $S_{v_{t+1}}$. Essentially, with rate adaption using AFR, a video analysis algorithm analyses every X^{th} frame in a video segment v_t instead of all the frames in every video segment in the video stream. While, with ARR, the video analysis algorithm analyses every video segment v_t with low to high resolution instead of analyzing the whole video stream at a constant high quality. Subsequently, the resulting frame rate and resolution used to analyze the current video segment dictates at what frame

---
Algorithm 2: AFR

---

1 **Function** AFR (S_{v_t},*c1*,*c2*):
2   Input video segment for analysis;
3   **if** $x_t \geq p_t$ **then**
4         $r_{t+1} = FrameRateArray\,[r_t - c1]$
5   **else**
6         $r_{t+1} = FrameRateArray\,[r_t + c2]$
7   **end**
8     $M_{t+1} = DictionaryNeuralNetworks\,[r_{t+1}]$ /* Key:FrameRate, Val:M_{t+1} */
9     $p_{t+1} = DictionaryThresholds\,[M_{t+1}]$ /* Key:M_t, Val:p_{t+1} */
10   PredictandUpdate(M_{t+1}, S_v) return $S_{v_{t+1}}$
11 **return**

Algorithm 3: ARR

---

1 **Function** ARR (S_{v_t},*c1*,*c2*):
2   Input video segment for analysis;
3   **if** $x_t \geq p_t$ **then**
4         $\rho_{t+1} = ResolutionsArray\,[\rho_t - c1]$
5   **else**
6         $\rho_{t+1} = ResolutionsArray\,[\rho_t + c2]$
7   **end**
8     $M_{t+1} = DictionaryNeuralNetworks\,[\rho_{t+1}]$ /* Key:Resolution, Val:M_{t+1} */
9     $p_{t+1} = DictionaryThresholds\,[M_{t+1}]$ /* Key:M_t, Val:p_{t+1} */
10   PredictandUpdate(M_{t+1}, S_v) return $S_{v_{t+1}}$
11 **return**

---

rate and resolution the video segment should be stored to optimally use the storage resources and reduce the cost of storage. The resulting frame rate and resolution used during analysis of the current video segment also dictates the frame rate and resolution of the next video segment to be uploaded to the Edge. In EVA, the video stream uploading module in the camera/device's API requests the frame rate and resolution for the next video segment to the video analysis module operating in the Edge. The resulting frame rate and resolution used during analysis of the current video segment (feedback) is sent back as the reply. This ensures an efficient use of the available bandwidth.

We assume that DNNs are stored in an increasing order of their complexity. Therefore, the DNNs can be easily accessed similar to accessing values in an array with the help of a reference index. We propose to adapt the frame rates and resolutions in AFR and ARR with the help of two counters c1 and c2 referred to as the decrement and increment indexes. We propose to use two counters to accommodate distinctive behaviours that need to be applied in selecting the DNNs when normal and abnormal activities are found in the videos. The rate adaption using these counters is described as follows:

The decrement counter is *'c1'* where $(0 < c1 < n)$ and increment counter is *'c2'* where $(0 < c2 < n)$. The DNN M_{t+1} for the video segment v_{t+1} is selected as follows:

$$M_{t+1}\left(v_{t+1}\right) = \begin{cases} r_\mathrm{i} - c1, \rho_i - c1 & if \quad x_t \geq p_t \\ r_\mathrm{i} + c2, \rho_i + c2 & Otherwise. \end{cases}$$

Essentially, upon finding normal activity in the current video segment, we decrease the frame rate/resolution for the next upcoming segment and select a DNN with the decrement counter 'c1'. Whereas, when abnormal activity is found, we increase the frame rate and the resolution for the next video segment and select a DNN with the increment counter 'c2'.

The basic idea of the rate adaption with AFR and ARR during video analysis is based on the prediction accuracy during the analysis of the previous video segment in time as shown in the Algorithms 2 and 3. Every video segment is basically a collection of frames that are at a specific resolution with temporal dependency among the frames. Based on the analysis of current video segment, with AFR the resolution remains constant, but the frame rate is increased for the next video segment if suspicious activity was detected in the current video segment (line 6: algorithm 2), and decreased if the detected (line 4: algorithm 2) normal content was above an acceptable threshold (*e.g.*, 75%). Similarly, with ARR the frame rate remains constant, while the resolution is increased for the next video segment if suspicious activity was detected in the current video segment (line 6: algorithm 3), and decreased (line 4: algorithm 3) if the detected normal content was above an acceptable threshold (*e.g.*, 75%).

As shown in the algorithm 1, we first select either AFR or ARR and then select the values for the counter c1 and c2 at the onset of the video analysis process and this remains constant during the analysis of the current video segment of a specified length used by the video analysis algorithm. If AFR is selected, then according to algorithm 2 and the counters c1 and c2, we find the frame rate r_{t+1} and the corresponding DNN M_{t+1} for the current video segment and perform predictions to classify the video segment into its respective category, *e.g.*, normal, shoplifting, *etc.* Similarly, if ARR is selected, then according to algorithm 3, and the counters c1 and c2, we find the resolution ρ_{t+1} and the corresponding DNN M_{t+1} and perform prediction. After the analysis, the resulting frame rate (r_{t+1}) and resolution (ρ_{t+1})

can be used by the storage module in Edge to decide the frame rate and resolution at which the current video segment will be stored in the Edge/Cloud. Subsequently, this feedback is used to dictate the upload frame rate and resolution of upcoming video segments as discussed earlier to efficiently utilize the bandwidth. In this chapter, the values for the counters 'c1' and 'c2' are set with an assumption that available DNNs can be accessed similar to an array as shown in line 4 and 6 in algorithm 2 and 3. Please note that, this can be changed (to suit) as per the needs of the implementation of the algorithm. The aim is to efficiently select a DNN from the set of available DNNs that can be accessed with the counters as reference indexes. The rationale to increase the frame rates in AFR and resolutions in ARR when the prediction degraded below the threshold is that DNNs with higher frame rates and resolutions process more data points and hence have more features to consider during analysis; thereby, improve the accuracy of prediction. Even though, this increases the resource consumption during video analysis, it is essential when abnormal activities are detected. This is also reflected by the results obtained with the baseline profiler from Awstream in §10.2 where, the profiler selected higher frame rates and resolutions as the optimal configurations to increase the accuracy of prediction.

9.5 Chapter summary

In this chapter, we studied video analysis application's requirements and observed that video analysis is the most time consuming, resource demanding and expensive operation. We proposed a distributed architecture named EVA to exploit the benefits of Edge and Cloud through identifying the minimum set of services needed to support the video surveillance applications at the Edge. Further, we also noticed that profiling adds additional overhead during video analysis. Hence, we proposed 2-stage deep learning to build efficient and robust DNNs that produced higher accuracies with minimal configurations and thereby, eliminated the need for profiling. We also proposed two rate adaptive algorithms: AFR and ARR to optimize the video analysis at Edge and efficiently utilize the available bandwidth and storage.

Chapter 10

Application - Video Analysis

With the technological advancements, cameras have become indispensable and have given rise to many new applications. One such prevalent application is the Video surveillance and Management Systems (VMS). The VMS applications store and analyze video sequences and their meta-data information associated with safety events. They detect potential and on-going security breaches like robbery and crime and take timely actions to prevent incidents like vehicular accidents, fire hazards, *etc.* These systems require many different services such as transcoding, video streaming, storage, analysis, *etc.* Since VMS usually record videos round the clock, they demand massive storage and bandwidth requirements. Further, analysis of such large data requires high-performance computing, which is expensive although essential. Therefore, in this chapter, we leverage the *UCF-Crime dataset* [61] to measure the performance of the DNNs built using the 2-stage deep learning and the rate adaption algorithms proposed in EVA from Chapter 9. The evaluations show that, EVA considerably outperforms the baseline Awstream algorithm with 71% improvements in resource consumption and 69% in CPU utilization whilst reducing the bandwidth consumption by 70% and storage by 61%.

Contents

10.1 Preliminary evaluation

In the preliminary evaluation we measured the performance of DNNs that were built using the proposed 2-stage deep learning technique.

10.1.1 Dataset

The UCF-Crime [61] dataset consists of real world surveillance videos representing 13 different anomalies: Normal, Shoplifting, Arrest, Burglary, Road Accident, Fighting, Explosion, Robbery, Arson, Stealing, Abuse, Shooting, Vandalism and Assault. The dataset also supplies the associated ground-truths for the videos. It was sufficient for us to just identify normal and abnormal activities in the videos during analysis to show the applicability of our solution and measure its benefits. Therefore, to reduce the overhead of the experiments we classified the videos into their individual respective classes and further into two broad classes namely: Normal and Abnormal. Please note that for simplicity, we only show the results with Normal and Abnormal classes. Since the videos in the original dataset were of uneven length, we merged them using a video joiner tool and split them into equal length videos of 1 minute segments. Subsequently, we created a dataset with 40 Normal and 90 Abnormal videos for evaluation. We further split the dataset into three smaller datasets for training (80%) and validating (10%) the DNNs in the offline stage and testing (10%) in the online stage.

10.1.2 Experimental setup

The training and experiments were performed on an Intel quad core based server with 100GB RAM and 350GB hard disk. The server located in the server room in a building was used to represent the Edge. A client camera with 100Mb/s link to the Edge was used for uploading the videos to the Edge for analysis. We envision that our solution can also be deployed on resource restrictive IoT Edge environments, hence, we performed the experiments with only CPU. However, we observed that, even without GPU, our proposed rate adaptive algorithms have outperformed the existing profiling techniques that demand expensive and additional computational resources. Therefore, we envision that our solution is also compatible for deployment on normal servers and even smaller network of embedded computing boards.

For the experiments, we selected five frame rates [152]: 6fps, 8fps, 10fps, 15fps and 30fps and three resolutions [153]: 240p (320x240p-Mobile quality), 480p (640x480p-TV quality) and 720p (1280x720p-HD) that are most commonly used in commercial applications [152,153]. The frame rates indicate the number of frames used per second while the resolutions indicate the number of pixels in every frame in the video.

10.1.3 2-stage deep learning

We implemented the DNNs in python and initially used the Keras [42] API version of Google's pre-trained InceptionV3 CNN network, which was trained using the Imagenet dataset. We used transfer learning to re-train the CNN network with its existing weights using Tensorflow framework to generate the sequences. We then used these sequences to build deep RNNs with LSTM architecture using the videos in the dataset.

While testing the DNNs, we computed accuracy of a video segment by comparing it against the ground truth if it is available such as in the offline case or by comparing it with the accuracy of the most expensive DNN configuration, *i.e.*, the *golden configuration* [31]. As discussed earlier in Chapter 9 §9.3, golden configurations are expensive, but they are known to produce high quality results. In this chapter, the golden configuration is built using DNNs with deepest layers that produced higher accuracy during training with all the frames in the videos at highest available resolution. During evaluation, we measure the prediction accuracy by leveraging the F1 score metric which is computed as the harmonic mean of precision and recall; where an F1 score of 0 represents the lowest and 1 represents the highest prediction accuracy. F1 scores are more commonly used in machine learning applications and our evaluations are consistent with prior works that use this metric [14,31,32]. Please note that, the proposed approach can also be used with other accuracy metrics.

10.1.3.1 Offline stage

During the offline training, we built a DNN for each selected frame rate and resolution. For DNNs with different frame rates, we maintained a constant resolution of 240p for the videos. Whereas, for building DNNs with different resolutions, we maintained a constant frame rate of 30fps for the videos. We used deep learning to build DNNs for each selected frame rate and resolution by starting with 1 layer and incrementally increasing it to 12, 16, 20, 30, 128, 256, 512 and 1024 layers. During training we split the 1min video segments into frames and passed the frames to the CNN model to extract features at the final pool layer. We then built a sequence from these extracted features and passed them to the LSTM RNN for training and subsequently predicted the class of the video segment *i.e.*, Normal or Abnormal. We started the training with a shallow DNN and increased its layers whenever there was a degradation in the observed prediction accuracy. We continued this process until we found a stable and deep enough DNN (1024 layer in our experiments) that produced higher accuracies. We validated the results from these DNNs with the ground-truth from the UCF-Crime dataset before deploying them in the online stage.

10.1.3.2 Online stage

During online stage, we sequentially uploaded the test videos to the Edge that were previously unseen by the DNNs during their offline training. Similar to the offline stage, the DNNs continuously trained themselves with the newer incoming videos and simultaneously analyzed them for any abnormal content. In online stage, to mimic a real world situation, we validated the prediction accuracy with the golden configuration as the ground truth for new videos would not be available. Since the ground truth from UCF-Crime dataset was also available, we further cross verified the prediction accuracy with the ground truth.

10.1.4 Prediction accuracy

Video analysis is expected to perform with high accuracy [14] especially when peoples lives are at risk such as in VMS. Hence, it is crucial to build DNNs that accurately classify videos as Normal or Abnormal based on their content. Further, in EVA, our goal is to eliminate the overhead of profiling. Therefore, we used a 2-stage approach to build DNNs with existing data in offline stage followed by continuous training in online stage to improve the performance of the DNNs.

We needed to ensure these DNNs produced predictions with high accuracy in both offline and online stage. Hence, we measured the prediction accuracy of these DNNs with the test data in offline stage using the ground truth. However, to measure the prediction accuracy, during online stage, we initialized the cameras with the videos from the dataset and started uploading them sequentially to the Edge for analysis.

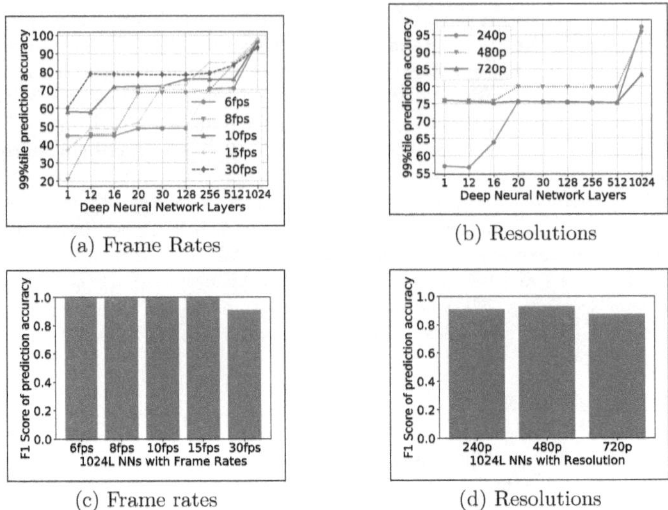

(a) Frame Rates   (b) Resolutions

(c) Frame rates   (d) Resolutions

Figure 10.1: Prediction accuracy of DNNs.

For each incoming video, we trained the DNN with the video and then predicted the class of the video as Normal or Abnormal. The prediction accuracy in online stage was validated using the golden configuration and further cross-validated with the ground-truth in the UCF-Crime dataset. The same experiment was repeated with all DNNs with different frame rates and resolutions. The resulting class and prediction accuracy for each video segment was recorded.

To select an optimal DNN for each selected frame rate and resolution, we compared the performance of DNN's with different number of layers and plotted a graph with the 99 percentile prediction accuracy as shown in Figure 10.1 (a) & (b). While, the F1 score for the deepest 1024 layer DNNs that were selected for AFR and ARR are shown in Figure 10.1 (c) & (d). We noticed from the results that with less layers the DNNs were too shallow and hence the predictions varied greatly and produced false positives. However, as we reached 128 layers, the predictions stabilized and steadily started to increase until we reached 1024 layers where we achieved higher accuracies of 93% - 98% with different frame rates and 83% - 97% with different resolutions. Moreover, the results show that DNN's with 1024 layers produced considerably high accuracies with high F1 scores for all frame rates and resolutions *i.e.*, even with just 6fps we obtained 96% accuracy and 240p produced 97% accuracy with ≈0.91 F1 score. We conclude from these results that with the 2-stage deep learning approach

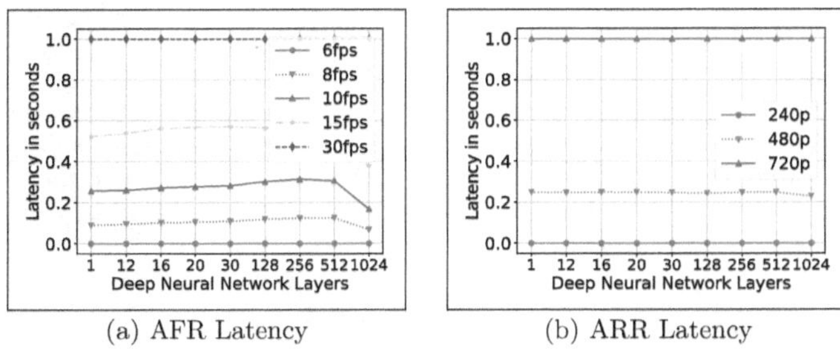

(a) AFR Latency   (b) ARR Latency

Figure 10.2: Latency.

we were able to build robust DNNs with high accuracies. Further, we used the actual data that needed to be inspected to continually train the DNNs during the online stage and the resulting DNNs were able to produce high accuracies and learn newer threat patterns instantly.

10.1.5 Latency

Cloud service providers are moving to the Edge in order to reduce latency [154]. Hence, it is crucial to evaluate the latency of prediction during video analysis. Therefore, we measured the prediction latency once the DNNs stabilized at 1024 layers. For this experiment, we randomly chose a video segment (1min length) from the dataset and placed it in the cameras. The cameras uploaded the video segment to the Edge for analysis. In the Edge, we analyzed the video segment with the DNNs built for the five different frame rates and three resolutions. We recorded the execution time for the prediction function during the experiments to represent the latency.

The results are shown in Figure 10.2. We observed from the results that, execution time of the prediction function increased linearly with increase in frame rates and resolutions *i.e.*, lower the frame rate and resolution, lower the latency of prediction. Combining the findings from Figure 10.1 and Figure 10.2, we conclude that DNNs with smaller frame rates (*e.g.*, 6fps) and low resolution (240p) can also produce accurate results (98%). Therefore, in EVA we propose to use lower frame rates and resolutions to analyze the videos when it has normal content and utilize higher frame rates and resolutions at the onset of discovering abnormal content. Consequently, leading to faster execution time; thereby, we can dramatically reduce the consumption of computing resources and speed up video analysis. This was a key finding that motivated us to propose the rate adaption algorithms.

10.2 Evaluation

The DNNs built using the proposed 2-stage deep learning in the preliminary evaluation (§10.1) are used in the remainder of this section to evaluate and compare AFR and ARR to the baseline Awstream approach. We especially measured the benefits achieved with the rate adaption algorithms w.r.t. resource utilization, bandwidth and storage.

10.2.1 Baseline

For comparing the performance of EVA with a baseline profiling technique, we consider the recently proposed Awstream approach by Zhang *et al.* [32]. Awstream, provides an API for the profiler to find the configurations that optimizes the WAN bandwidth and improves the accuracy of prediction. However, Awstream essentially fine tunes the application knobs during object detection in images. Therefore, we implemented the Awstream profiling techniques for video analysis with DNNs.

10.2.2 Experimental setup

After ensuring that DNNs predicted with the desired accuracy (§10.1.4) and latency (§10.1.5), we used the 1024 layer DNNs to analyze and compare AFR and ARR with the best and least performing settings dictated by the counters c1 and c2 (See §9.4). For simplicity we name the best performing setting as *additive* where c1 and c2 select the available DNNs in an increment and decrement fashion sequentially. While the least performing setting is named as *multiplicative* since the counter c2 increments in a multiplicative fashion upon detecting anomalies while c1 decrements sequentially. For the baseline profiling technique with Awstream, we allowed the profiler to select the most optimal DNN configurations from the available set of configurations with different frame rates and resolutions for analyzing each video segment.

For the following experiments, we prepared a combination of 11 Normal video segments (NV) and Abnormal video segments (AV) in the following order 1-NV, 2-4AV, 5-7NV, 8-9AV, 10-11NV and the cameras uploaded them in the given order to the Edge for analysis. During analysis, we selected 8fps DNN for AFR and 240p DNN for ARR as the benchmarks since they had high prediction accuracy with lower latency. We set the threshold for normal content in the video to 75% based on our testing during the offline stage and following the recommendation from Loewenherz *et al.* [155] where they found that F1 score of ≥ 0.7 (70%) was a good indicator in analytic applications.

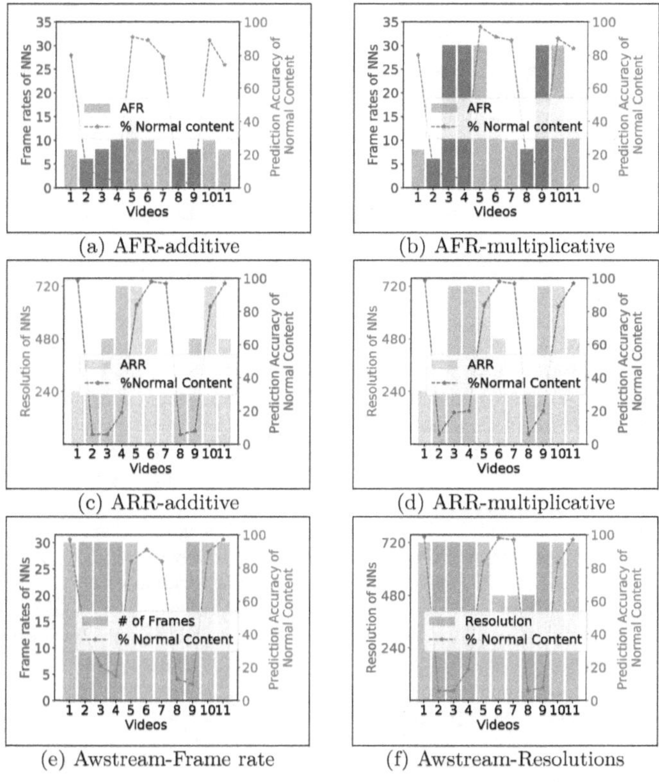

Figure 10.3: **Comparison of AFR, ARR and Awstream.**

10.2.3 Adaptive rate algorithms

We used the AFR and ARR algorithms (algorithm 2 & 3 from Chapter 9 §9.4) and selectively initialized the video analysis with additive variant followed by multiplicative variant. We also set the rate adaption counters c1 and c2 to 1 in additive stage and c1=1 and c2=n-a, in multiplicative stage where n is the number of available DNNs; one DNN for each frame rate in AFR and each resolution in ARR and 'a' is the index of the current DNN. During the experiment, for each of the 11 videos, we recorded the frame rates and resolutions used during their analysis and the resulting prediction accuracy of the normal content detected in the video. The results for AFR are shown in Figure 10.3(a) & (b) and the results for ARR are shown in Figure 10.3(c) & (d) while the results for the baseline profiling technique in Awstream are shown in Figure 10.3(e) & (f)

10.2.3.1 AFR

Essentially, the AFR algorithm decreased the frame rate during success (normal) and increased the frame rate during failure (abnormal activities like, shoplifting). Whereas, the baseline profiling technique in Awstream, picked the most optimal DNN configuration for analyzing each video segment. As seen from the results in Figure 10.3(a) & (b), during the experiment, the AFR algorithm with both additive and multiplicative modes analyzed the first video segment with 8fps DNN, and predicted that normal content was 80% ($\geq$75%). Since the prediction passed the threshold with normal content $\geq$75%, the algorithm assumed there was no abnormal activity. Hence, AFR decreased the frame rate as indicated by the sequential decrement counter 'c1' and predicted the second video segment with 6fps DNN with both additive and multiplicative modes. However, since the second video segment was an abnormal video segment, the algorithm predicted only 11% normal content. Since the prediction accuracy failed to achieve $\geq$75% normal content, the algorithm increased the frame rate as indicated by the counter 'c2' with sequential increment in additive stage and multiplicative increment in multiplicative stage. Therefore the third video segment was analyzed with 8fps DNN with additive stage and 30fps DNN with multiplicative stage. This continued until AFR processed the 5th video segment where it predicted normal content was 91% and started decreasing the frame rate by the counter 'c1' and subsequently analyzed 6th video segment with 10fps DNN with additive stage and 15fps DNN with multiplicative stage and so on.

The results for the baseline Awstream profiler for selecting the optimal DNN configuration at multiple frame rates are shown in Figure 10.3(e). The same experiment as AFR was repeated with the Awstream profiler, which selected the deepest DNN with 1024 layers with the highest available frame rate of 30fps for eight out of 11 video segments and second highest frame rate of 15fps for the remaining 3 video segments.

10.2.3.2 ARR

Similar to AFR, the ARR algorithm decreased the resolutions during success (normal) and increased the resolution during failure (abnormal events like shoplifting). As seen from the results in Figure 10.3(c) & (d), during the experiment, the ARR algorithm with both additive and multiplicative modes, analyzed the first video seg-

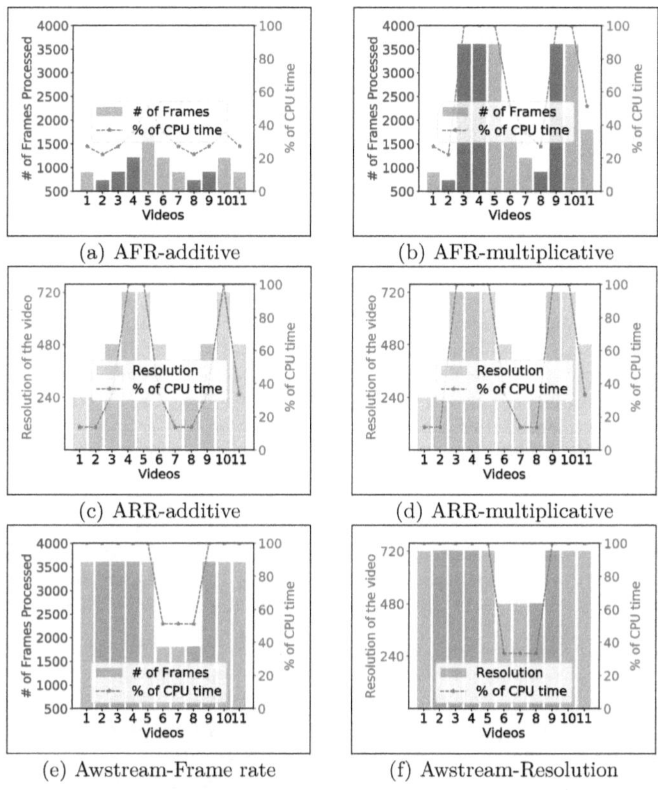

Figure 10.4: **Resources used in AFR, ARR and Awstream.**

ment with 240p DNN, and predicted that normal content was 99% ($\geq$75%). Since the prediction passed the threshold with normal content $\geq$75%, the algorithm assumed there was no abnormal activity. Hence, ARR decreased the resolution as indicated by the sequential decrement counter 'c1', but since 240p is the lowest available resolution, the algorithm predicted the second video segment with 240p DNN with both additive and multiplicative modes. However, since the second video segment was an abnormal video segment, the algorithm predicted only 6% normal content. Since the prediction accuracy failed to achieve $\geq$75% normal content, the algorithm increased the resolution as indicated by the counter 'c2' with sequential increment in additive

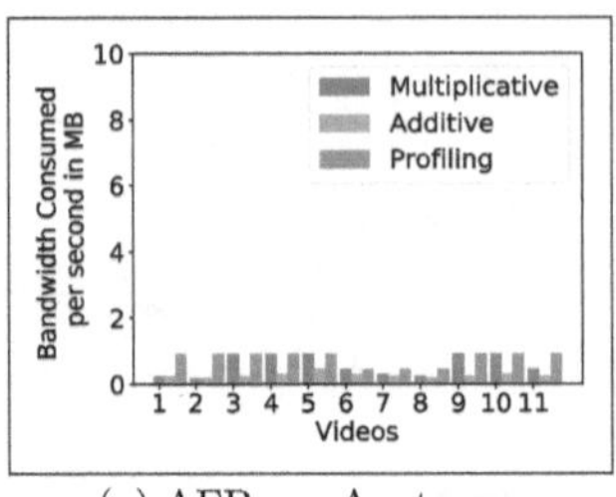
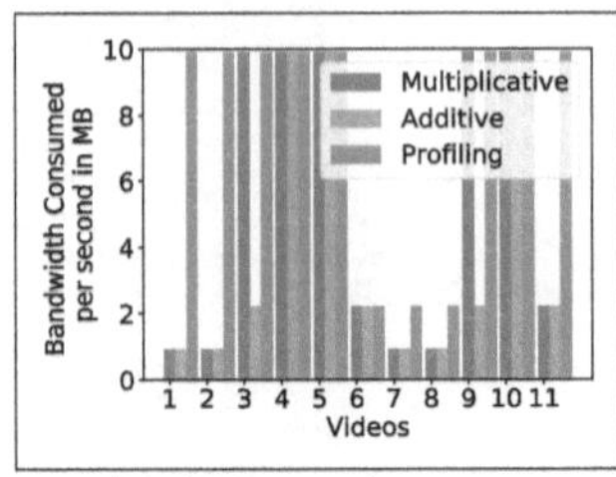

(a) AFR vs. Awstream   (b) ARR vs. Awstream

Figure 10.5: **Comparison of bandwidth.**

stage and multiplicative increment in multiplicative stage. Therefore, the third video segment was analyzed with 480p DNN with additive stage and 720p DNN with multiplicative stage. This continued until ARR processed the 5th video segment where it predicted normal content was 84% and started decreasing the resolution as indicated by the sequential decrement counter 'c1' and subsequently analyzed 6th video segment with 480p DNN with additive and multiplicative stage and so on.

The results for the Awstream profiler for selecting the optimal DNN configuration with different resolutions are shown in Figure 10.3(f). The same experiment as ARR was repeated with the Awstream profiler, which selected the deepest DNN with 1024 layers with the highest available resolution of 720p for eight out of 11 video segments and second highest resolution of 480p for the remaining 3 video segments.

As observed from the results in Figure 10.3(a)-(d), in EVA, AFR and ARR used higher frame rate and higher resolution DNNs only when abnormal activity was detected, and lower frame rate and lower resolution DNNs were used whenever normal activity was detected. However, in comparison, the results in Figure 10.3(e)&(f) show that baseline Awstream profiler used the DNNs with best configurations and ended up with higher frame rates and resolutions as a trade-off for improving accuracy. Moreover, in both AFR and ARR, we noticed a much smoother transition among DNNs with the best settings for counter values 'c1' and 'c2' in additive stage in comparison to multiplicative stage. Therefore, multiplicative stage was more computationally intensive than additive stage. However, even with the least optimal configuration, rate adaption algorithms performed better than the baseline Awstream.

10.2.4 Resource consumption

Authors in [14,32] show that substantial amount of resources are needed to host the DNNs and speed up video analysis. Therefore, we used the same experiment for AFR

132

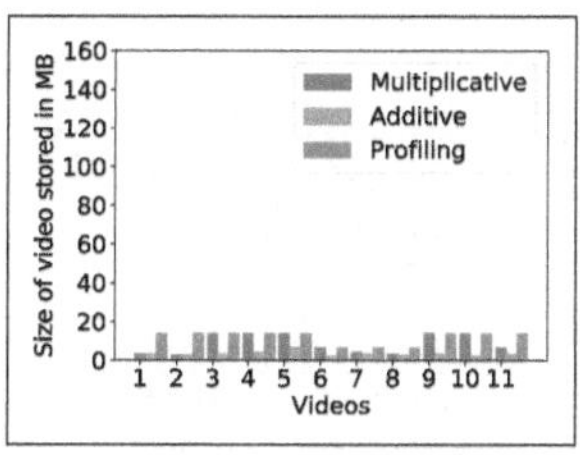
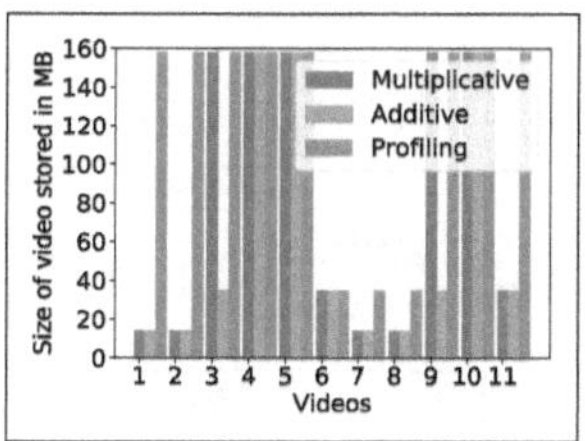

(a) AFR vs. Awstream   (b) ARR vs. Awstream

Figure 10.6: **Comparison of storage.**

(§ 10.2.3.1) and ARR (§ 10.2.3.2) to measure the benefits w.r.t. processing, storage and bandwidth in comparison to the baseline profiling technique in Awstream. A summary of these findings are given in the Table 10.1.

10.2.4.1 Processing

To verify the resource consumption w.r.t. processing, we measured the percentage of CPU time used for prediction. In addition, we measured the number of frames processed for each video segment in AFR and Awstream with different frame rates and the resolution of the video segments processed in ARR and Awstream with different resolutions. The results for AFR with additive and multiplicative modes are shown in Figure 10.4 (a) & (b) and the results for ARR with additive and multiplicative modes are shown in Figure 10.4 (c) & (d) while the results for profiling with Awstream are show in Figure 10.4 (e) & (f) respectively. We observed from the figures that, DNNs with lower frame rates and lower resolutions noticeably consumed less resources. Since with additive and multiplicative modes we were able to efficiently utilize the optimal DNNs for every video segment, we unmistakably saved a lot of computational resources in comparison to the resources consumed by Awstream. Further, we also compared additive stage with multiplicative stage and observed that rate adaption in additive stage performed better than multiplicative stage and provided greater savings in terms of CPU utilization, frame rates and resolution.

10.2.4.2 Bandwidth

To examine the bandwidth consumption, we measured the amount of bandwidth used by each video segment that was uploaded to the Edge for analysis. The uploading frame rates and resolutions were based on the feedback received from the analysis of prior video segments in time using AFR and ARR. In Figure 10.5 (a)

133

Table 10.1: **Improvements with AFR, ARR and Awstream.**

Method	Processing	CPU	Storage	Bandwidth
AFR-additive	**71.36%**	**69.45%**	**73.88%**	**70.60%**
AFR-multiplicative	30.06%	35.12%	36.06%	35.75%
ARR-additive	**36.36%**	**55.54%**	**61.41%**	**61.22%**
ARR-multiplicative	30.30%	43.45%	47.27%	47.09%
AFR vs. ARR	**66.66%**	**86.23%**	**91.11%**	**90.66%**
Awstream-Frame	13.63%	13.31%	13.64%	13.63%
Awstream-Resolution	9.09%	18.13%	21.21%	12.20%

& (b) we summarized the bandwidth consumed by AFR and ARR with additive and multiplicative modes in comparison to baseline Awstream respectively. We observed that, there was an exponential increase in the bandwidth consumption as we increased the frame rates and resolutions of the DNNs. Further, we also compared additive and multiplicative modes and observed that additive stage consumed far less bandwidth than multiplicative stage. However, both additive and multiplicative modes outperformed the bandwidth consumed by the baseline Awstream.

10.2.4.3 Storage

In order to monitor the storage, we measured the size of each frame in each video segment as they were uploaded to the Edge for analysis with AFR, ARR and Awstream. Using the feedback for the frame rate and resolution obtained during video analysis with multiplicative and additive modes for each video segment, we gathered the amount of storage needed for that video segment with the frame rate selected by AFR and Awstream and resolution selected by ARR and Awstream. The resulting storage for the videos are shown in Figure 10.6 (a) & (b). It is evident from the results that whenever lower frame rate and lower resolution were used during video analysis, the corresponding demand for the needed storage also reduced in comparison to existing approaches that store full size videos. Once again we observed that additive stage demanded far less storage compared to multiplicative stage and both additive and multiplicative modes outperformed the baseline Awstream.

In this Chapter, with extensive evaluations we demonstrated the benefits of AFR and ARR in comparison to stae-of-the-art baseline profiling techniques like Awstream. A summary of the evaluations is listed in the Table 10.1. The following are the key takeaways from the evaluations:

(i) Overall, we were able to improve the resource consumption (*i.e.*, overall processed frames and resolutions) by 71%, CPU utilization by 69% and bandwidth utilization by 71% with 74% less storage in comparison to the existing profiling techniques. It is noticeable that AFR and ARR performed better with additive stage in comparison to multiplicative stage. This is because with multiplicative stage, AFR and ARR drastically raise their frame rates and resolution but have a smoother degradation and hence the improvements are relatively low compared to rate adaption using additive stage. However, both additive and multiplicative modes significantly outperformed the baseline profiling techniques.

(ii) AFR performed overwhelmingly better than ARR. This is intuitive as in ARR the DNNs adapt among resolutions whereas in AFR they adapt among frame rates *i.e.*, videos with multiple frame rates but a constant resolution are smaller in size and hence require less resources in comparison to videos with multiple resolutions.

(iii) AFR and ARR with multiplicative stage are more suitable for safety-critical applications like surveillance in airports, traffic-accidents, *etc.* Whereas, AFR and ARR with additive stage are more suitable for monitoring warehouses, factory floors, *etc.* Further, AFR is the obvious choice among the two rate adaption algorithms as it produced the best results w.r.t all metrics in this study.

(iv) Even though AFR is the obvious choice, with an increasing trend toward high resolution videos [63], we believe that based on applications requirements, ARR will also serve as a good candidate and can substantially contribute towards reducing the overall cost of operation during video analysis in comparison to existing profiling based approaches.

10.3 Chapter summary

In this chapter, we evaluated the 2-stage deep learning and rate adaptive algorithms proposed in EVA in Chapter 9 using the UCF-Crime dataset. With preliminary evaluations we demonstrated that, DNNs built using 2-stage deep learning produced higher accuracies with minimal latency. In addition, through evaluations of AFR and ARR we demonstrated 71% improvement in resource consumption whilst using 69% less CPU and 71% less bandwidth with 74% less storage compared to the state-of-the-art baseline solutions. Thus with a distributed architecture and 2-stage deep learning with rate adaption in EVA, we not only optimized the performance of video analysis using DNNs with EVA but also reduced the cost of the overall system through efficient utilization of the resources at the Edge and the available bandwidth.

Chapter 11

ADA: Adaptive Deep Log Anomaly Detector

Large private and government networks are often subjected to attacks like data extrusion and service disruption. Existing anomaly detection systems use offline supervised learning and employ experts for labeling. Hence they cannot detect anomalies in real-time. Even though unsupervised algorithms are increasingly used nowadays, they cannot readily adapt to newer threats. Moreover, many such systems also suffer from high cost of storage and require extensive computational resources. In this chapter, we propose ADA: Adaptive Deep Log Anomaly Detector, an unsupervised online DNN framework that leverages LSTM networks and regularly adapts to newer log patterns to ensure accurate anomaly detection. In ADA, an adaptive model selection strategy is designed to choose pareto-optimal configurations to efficiently utilize the resources. Further, a dynamic threshold algorithm is proposed to dictate the optimal threshold based on recently detected events to improve the detection accuracy. In addition, we use the predictions to guide the storage of abnormal data and effectively reduce the overall storage cost.

The key contributions in this work include:

- A novel unsupervised anomaly detection framework *ADA: Deep Adaptive Anomaly Detector*, which utilizes online deep learning to build highly accurate models on the fly. ADA also incorporates new log patterns instantly in order to improve anomaly detection.
- An adaptive prediction strategy for selecting the pareto-optimal ADA Event Model (ADA-EM) to optimize the computational resources and improve the latency during anomaly detection.
- A dynamic threshold computation technique for re-examining and improving

the threshold of DNN models for detecting anomalies.

- A proposal to leverage the insight from event predictions to redirect storage decisions in order to reduce the overall cost of storage.

Contents

11.1 System design

In this section, we introduce the design goals and rationale for design choices in ADA followed by the framework.

11.1.1 Design goals

The design of ADA is driven by the following main goals:

1) **Heterogeneous data:** System logs from various applications and systems are heterogeneous in nature and vary significantly in terms of their format and collected information. A generalized anomaly detection system should be able to process and analyze any log format.

2) **Supervision and Data drift:** System behavior and potential threats evolve over time. As a consequence, the system logs and attack models also change. An anomaly detection system should be able to learn newer event patterns automatically even in the absence of experts input and labelled dataset.

3) **Accuracy and Threshold:** Anomaly detection systems should correctly predict the abnormal events with high accuracy. In addition, it should adapt

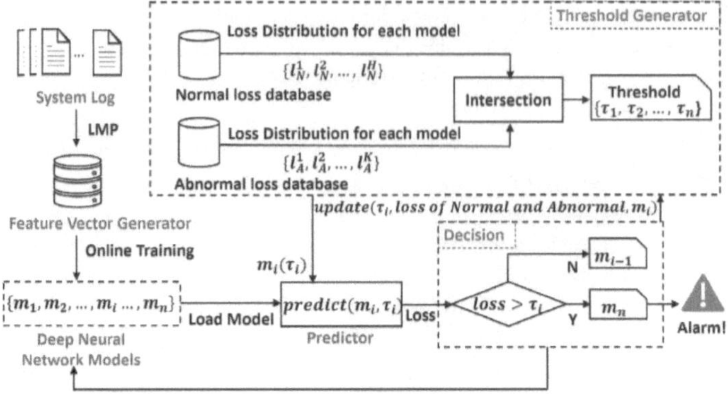

Figure 11.1: **ADA architecture.**

system thresholds based on recently observed events and system behaviour to clearly distinguish between normal and abnormal events and reduce false negatives.

4) **Resource utilization:** Since many anomaly detection systems are based on DNNs, they demand high computational resources to produce higher accuracy and use parallelization to reduce latency. An efficient anomaly detection system should be able to use modern and established algorithms with minimal resources.

5) **Cost:** System logs are generated everyday and hence the storage cost for these logs also increases with time. An efficient strategy for storage can greatly reduce the overall storage cost. Further, many offline algorithms also use increased computational resources to improve the accuracy. An anomaly detection system should be able to produce results with good resource-accuracy trade-off.

11.1.2 Architectural components

Figure 11.1 shows the ADA framework in detail. The components of this framework are described as follows:

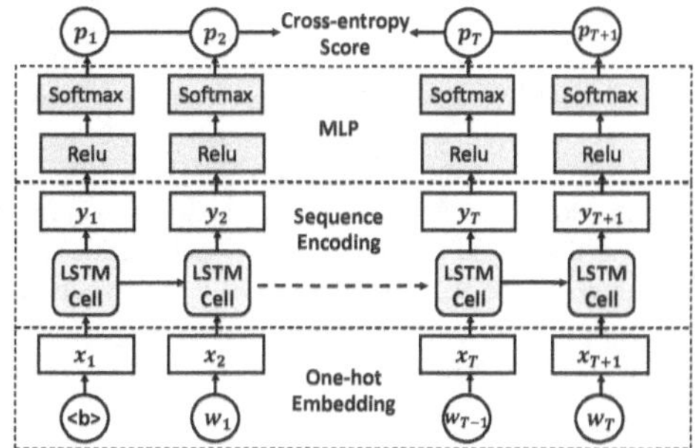

Figure 11.2: **ADA Event Model.**

- <u>System Logs:</u> This module stores and feeds the logs to the Feature Vector Generator module. The logs are collected from multiple sources in the system and contains information about different system states and events of interest defined by the system administrators.

- <u>Feature Vector Generator:</u> This module uses the Language Model Processing (LMP) [156] to process incoming log streams and generates feature vectors. The resulting features are stored in the feature vector database.

- <u>Models:</u> This module generates online DNNs using the ADA-EM shown in Figure 11.2 for detecting anomalies in system logs.

- <u>Predictor:</u> This module initially uses the benchmark model m_i for predicting the incoming log event and sends the prediction results to the decision module. Based on the prediction and adaptive principle shown in algorithm 4 (see §11.1.5), the corresponding next model will be loaded and used for predicting the next event.

- <u>Decision:</u> This module uses the prediction from the predict module and decides whether the predicted event is a normal or abnormal event using algorithm 4.

- <u>Threshold Generator:</u> This module stores the recent normal event losses $\{l_N^1, l_N^2, \cdots, l_N^H\}$ and abnormal event losses $\{l_A^1, l_A^2, \cdots, l_A^K\}$ for each model m_i. Using the dynamic threshold computation (see §11.2), we obtain the current threshold for every model.

11.1.3 Tokenization

In order to readily use the arbitrary log formats, we treat every line in the log file as a sequence of tokens. In this chapter, we consider word-level tokenization granularity in log files. For tokenizing the words, we assume that the tokens in every line in the log are delimited by some known characters (e.g., a space, a comma or a period). We split every ine in the log file based on the delimiter and define a shared vocabulary of "words" over all fields in the log file. Essentially, the vocabulary is composed of the most frequently appearing tokens in the system logs. Further, we treat any missing data as a single feature and use the character "?" to represent it.

11.1.4 ADA Event Model (ADA-EM)

In order to efficiently implement the ADA framework, we also propose ADA-EM shown in Figure 11.2 leveraging LSTM networks. The LSTM architecture was first introduced for machine translation in [157] and since then it has been extensively applied in language processing applications. Therefore, we train the LSTM-based ADA-EM to process instances of normal time-series in the system logs. Specifically, ADA-EM takes the embedded sequences of tokens as input and outputs the distribution for the next token.

We begin with one-hot embedding, which produces unique embedding vectors for every token in the vocabulary set. More specifically, suppose we have a line in the log file with T tokens, and we can describe it as $\mathcal{W} = \{w_0, w_1, \cdots, w_T\}$ where w_0 represents the starting flag $\langle b \rangle$ followed by T tokens of the log line. The layer of one-hot embedding processes the time-series log-line input with $T+1$ tokens $\mathcal{W}$ into one-hot vectors $\mathcal{X} = \{\mathbf{x}_0, \mathbf{x}_1, \cdots, \mathbf{x}_{T+1}\}$.

The one-hot embedding is followed by the sequence encoding. Among such large amount of normal events in logs, there exists potential sequential information for language models. To capture this sequential information, an improved LSTM is used in ADA-EM, which is well suited for this task. When applying LSTM recursively to a line in the event log from left to right, the sequence representation will be enhanced progressively with the information from subsequent tokens in this sequence.

Based on the input one-hot vectors, LSTM produces the summary of the past input sequences through the cell state vector $\mathbf{c}_t$. Given $\mathcal{X}$, $\mathbf{y}_t$ is the hidden state of the LSTM cell at time t, which can help to achieve the desired log event prediction. After T times of recursive updates from Eqs. (11.1) to (11.5), the hidden representation at token t namely y_t gives a better representation of each token.

$$\mathbf{y}_t = \mathbf{o}_t \circ tanh(\mathbf{c}_t), \tag{11.1}$$

$$\mathbf{c}_t = \mathbf{f}_t \circ \mathbf{c}_{t-1} + \mathbf{i}_t \circ tanh(\mathbf{W}_{xc}\mathbf{x}_t + \mathbf{W}_{yc}\mathbf{y}_{t-1} + \mathbf{b}_c), \tag{11.2}$$

$$\mathbf{o}_t = \sigma(\mathbf{W}_{xo}\mathbf{x}_t + \mathbf{W}_{yo}\mathbf{y}_{t-1} + \mathbf{b}_o), \tag{11.3}$$

$$\mathbf{i}_t = \sigma(\mathbf{W}_{xi}\mathbf{x}_i + \mathbf{W}_{yi}\mathbf{y}_{t-1} + \mathbf{b}_i), \tag{11.4}$$

$$\mathbf{f}_t = \sigma(\mathbf{W}_{xf}\mathbf{x}_f + \mathbf{W}_{yf}\mathbf{y}_{t-1} + \mathbf{b}_f). \tag{11.5}$$

After that, a fully connected layer with final output unit of vocabulary size produces the output of the model. Once the hidden representations $\mathcal{Y} = \{\mathbf{y}_1, \mathbf{y}_2, \cdots, \mathbf{y}_{T+1}\}$ is obtained, we input these vectors into a Multi-Layer Perception (MLP) [158] and get the final probability distribution of the next token. Please note that we use two layers of MLP to achieve better representation capacity in ADA-EM. We use the ReLU activation function for the first layer in order to avoid over-fitting while the softmax function is used for the second layer to normalize the output of MLP layer and get the target output. Given the weight metrics $\mathbf{W}_r, \mathbf{W}_s$ and bias vectors $\mathbf{b}_r, \mathbf{b}_s$ for these two layers, the target output $\mathbf{p}_t$ can be formulated as follows:

$$\mathbf{p}_t = \text{softmax}(\mathbf{b}_s + \mathbf{W}_s(\text{Relu}(\mathbf{b}_r + \mathbf{W}_r(\mathbf{y}_t)))).$$

We use $\frac{1}{T}\sum_{t=1}^{T} H(\mathbf{x}_{t+1}, \mathbf{p}_t)$ as the cross-entropy loss function along with resources in ADA-EM for two important purposes: for obtaining an anomaly score for every log line and as the training objective to update the model weights.

11.1.5 ADA design

ADA is basically an event driven anomaly detection framework that detects abnormal events in system logs. With an assumption that initial training logs at the first hour represents normal behavior we begin the online training to build DNN models similar to Doyen et. al [64]. We start by building a shallow LSTM model using the normal log data from the 1st hour. As the time progresses, the number of models also increase with each model having deeper layers than the previous model in time. The goal is to build a DNN model from the captured logs in real-time and at the same time use the model to predict any anomalies in the logs. We acknowledge

Algorithm 4: Adaptive decision making algorithm

1 Input: Initialize Pareto-optimal model m_i with its configuration c_i and threshold τ_i
2 Output: Decision, loss
3 Decision = unknown
4 for *Each log event $d \in D$* **do**
5   loss = Predict(m_i, d)
6   **if** *loss $\leq \tau_i$* **then**
7   select m_{i-1}
8   Decision = Normal
9   **else**
10   select m_n
11   Decision = Abnormal
12   **end**
13 end
14 return Decision, loss

that at the beginning when the model is not trained well, high false positives are observed, however, as we build deeper models, the accuracy gets better over time. Further, models can be added or updated according to the variations observed during predictions. For instance, during the first four hours, we generated a model m_1 with 128 LSTM layers and this model produced a F1-score of ~91% (see §12.1). With the increasing number of log samples, the number of layers was also increased and we generated a second model m_2 with 258 layers which produced an F1-score of ~93%. This process is repeated until a deep enough model that produces the desired highest accuracy is obtained. We sort all the generated models based on their depth and represent them as a set $\{m_1, m_2, \cdots, m_n\}$ hereafter.

In ADA, every model in the model set is assigned a corresponding threshold value (see §11.2) for distinguishing the normal events from abnormal events. During decision making we use the algorithm 4, and every prediction is measured against the threshold for normal events established for the model. When an abnormal event is detected, the system immediately raises an alarm. The resulting decision drives the next model that should be used for predicting the next event in the log. By virtue of the adaptive principle as described in algorithm 4, whenever a normal event is found we select a model that is shallower than the current model and a deeper model otherwise. The resulting prediction loss is forwarded to the threshold generator for any required updates.

In this chapter, we define an event as the operational unit of work for any system

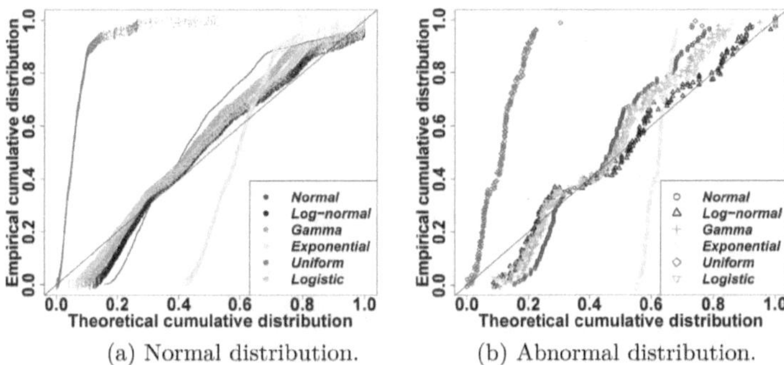

(a) Normal distribution.   (b) Abnormal distribution.

Figure 11.3: Loss distribution fit.

process which has a finite set of action sequences. Suppose that we have a set of DNN models where each model m_i has n_x layers. Each model m_i has one configuration $c_i, i \in n$. $\mathcal{C}$ is the set of all possible configurations of the models, $\mathcal{C} = \{c_1, c_2, \cdots, c_n\}$. For each configuration of c_i, we have two interested mappings: a mapping from c_i to its computation resource $R(c_i)$ and to its latency measure $T(c_i)$. ADA searches for Pareto-optimal set $\mathbb{P}$, such that there is no alternative model $m_i^{'}$ with a configuration $c_i^{'}$ that requires less computational resources (R) and offers lower latency (T). Formally, $\mathbb{P}$ is defined as follows:

$$\mathbb{P} = \{c_i \in \mathcal{C} : \{c_i^{'} \in \mathcal{C} : R(c_i^{'}) < R(c_i), T(c_i^{'}) < T(c_i)\} = \varnothing\}$$

As mentioned before, we treat log-lines as sequence of tokens and ADA learns normal behavior for a set of users who produced a stream of system logs as follows:

1) When a log stream arrives, the language processing model (LMP) is first utilized to abstract the tokens and build the log feature vector.

2) The above discussed pareto-optimal policy is used to select the optimal model m_i for the current system state.

3) The next model is selected by the feedback of prediction results from the current model following the algorithm 4. If the prediction result is normal, we select m_{i-1} which is the pareto-optimal model as it is shallower than current model and hence uses less computation and incurs less latency. Otherwise,

143

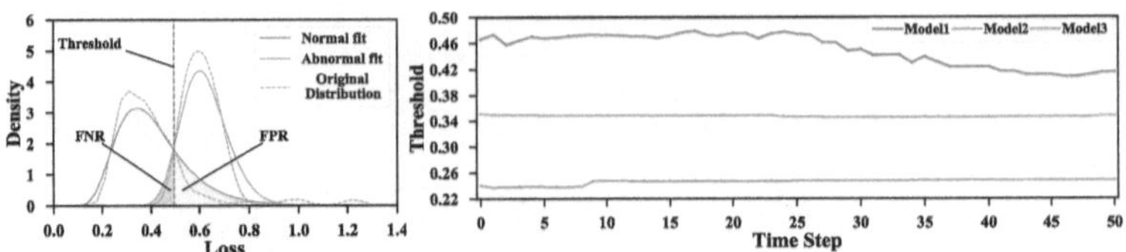

(a) Log normal distribution. (b) Threshold update over time steps.

Figure 11.4: **ADA dynamic threshold.**

the model m_n which is the deepest available model is chosen as it provides higher accuracy and is desired when an abnormal event is detected at the cost of increased computation.

4) The threshold τ is selected for each model based on the loss distribution of normal and abnormal data processed by the model and is discussed in the following section.

11.2 Threshold computation

The behavioural patterns in system logs change over time as newer threats and attacks are introduced to the system. Thus, predetermined threshold for normal and abnormal behaviours become inadequate and need to be updated regularly. Therefore, in this chapter we introduce a new dynamic threshold computation technique that automatically learns from the on-going behaviours in the system and adjusts the corresponding threshold for detecting anomalies.

Essentially, we inspect the loss distribution of logged events to automatically determine the threshold for every ADA-EM model. During the initial phase, for instance, the first hour, we only have normal log loss distribution and hence in order to compute the initial threshold we use a small number of abnormal events ground truth from the LANL dataset. Subsequently, once the models are introduced to more incoming events, the initial threshold and the loss distribution of normal and abnormal events are updated dynamically to reflect the observed behaviour in the log stream.

We studied several classical loss distributions and employed the Probability-Probability (P-P) plot to assess the appropriate fit for LANL dataset and find the optimal distribution for determining the threshold. In Figure 11.3, we plot the empirical distribution of losses obtained from the ADA-EM models against the best fitting theoretical distributions. From this figure, we can clearly see that for both normal and abnormal loss distributions, log normal is the best fit. Therefore, in ADA, we consider that log loss data follows the log normal distribution. In Figure 11.4(a) we show the losses with log-normal distribution for randomly chosen 10000 normal and 200 abnormal log events from the dataset. It is clear that point of intersection of both fits yields the best threshold choice in Figure 11.4(a), as the sum of True Positive Rate (TPR) and False Positive Rate (FPR) are minimum (see Proposition 1).

Definition 1. *For both normal and abnormal losses obtained by the ADA-EM models, the loss distributions are fitted by log normal distribution. Hence, the probability density function of real log data $p^{loss}(x)$ can be estimated by log normal density function $f^{\mu,\sigma}(x)$:*

$$p^{loss}(x) \approx f^{\mu,\sigma}(x),$$

where,

$$f^{\mu,\sigma}(x) = \frac{1}{\sqrt{2\pi}\sigma x} exp(-\frac{(log(x)-\mu)^2}{2\sigma^2}), x > 0.$$

The parameter μ and σ are estimated via maximum likelihood estimation based on the loss dataset. The challenge now is to find an optimal threshold based on the fits of losses. The loss threshold finding problem can be cast as the optimization problem formulated below,

$$\min_x \mathcal{L}(x) = (1 - F_X^N(x)) + F_X^A(x), x > 0, \tag{11.6}$$

where $F_X^N(x)$ and $F_X^A(x)$ are the Cumulative Distribution Function (CDF) of log-normal distribution [159] and X is the variable while x is the loss value of the variable X.

Proposition 1. *Two different log-normal densities always have an overlapping section with the condition that $\beta^2 - 4\alpha\gamma \geq 0$, where $\alpha = \frac{1}{2\sigma_2^2} - \frac{1}{2\sigma_1^2}$, $\beta = \frac{\mu_2}{2\sigma_2^2} - \frac{\mu_1}{2\sigma_1^2}$ and $\gamma = \frac{\mu_2}{2\sigma_2^2} - \frac{\mu_1}{2\sigma_1^2} - log(\frac{\sigma_1}{\sigma_2})$. The loss threshold $x \in \{x_1, x_2\}$ that satisfies the Eq. (11.6) is the optimal loss threshold x^*, where x_1 and x_2 are intersections of both log normal fits $f_N^{\mu_1,\sigma_1}(x)$ and $f_A^{\mu_2,\sigma_2}(x)$.*

Proof 1. *Let μ_1, σ_1 and μ_2, σ_2, where $\sigma_1, \sigma_2 > 0$, be the corresponding parameters of the density functions. Then*

$$\frac{1}{\sqrt{2\pi}\sigma_1 x} exp\left(-\frac{(log(x)-\mu_1)^2}{2\sigma_1^2}\right) = \frac{1}{\sqrt{2\pi}\sigma_2 x} exp\left(-\frac{(log(x)-\mu_2)^2}{2\sigma_2^2}\right).$$

$$\tag{11.7}$$

Applying the logarithm to Eq. (11.7), we have,

$$log(\frac{\sigma_1}{\sigma_2}) - (-\frac{(log(x) - \mu_2)^2}{2\sigma_2^2}) + (-\frac{(log(x) - \mu_1)^2}{2\sigma_1^2}) = 0. \tag{11.8}$$

Eq. (11.8) can be written in terms of a quadratic function in $log(x)$,

$$\alpha(log(x))^2 + \beta log(x) + \gamma = 0, \tag{11.9}$$

where $\alpha = \frac{1}{2\sigma_2^2} - \frac{1}{2\sigma_1^2}$, $\beta = \frac{\mu_2}{2\sigma_2^2} - \frac{\mu_1}{2\sigma_1^2}$ and $\gamma = \frac{\mu_2^2}{2\sigma_2^2} - \frac{\mu_1^2}{2\sigma_1^2} - log(\frac{\sigma_1}{\sigma_2})$.

Now, according to Definition 1, $\mathcal{L}(x)$ can be written in,

$$\begin{aligned}
\mathcal{L}(x) &= (1 - F_X^N(x)) + (F_X^A(x)) \\
&= P_N(X \geq x) + P_A(X \leq x) \\
&= \int_x^\infty f_N^{\mu_1,\sigma_1}(x) + \int_0^x f_A^{\mu_2,\sigma_2}(x).
\end{aligned} \tag{11.10}$$

Since $f^{\mu,\sigma}(x)$ is the continuous function in interval $(0, +\infty)$, the first order partial derivative of $\mathcal{L}(x)$ with respect to x, for $x > 0$, is given as,

$$\begin{aligned}
\frac{\partial \mathcal{L}(x)}{\partial x} &= -f_N^{\mu_1,\sigma_1}(x) + f_A^{\mu_2,\sigma_2}(x) \\
&= -\frac{1}{\sqrt{2\pi}\sigma_1 x} exp(-\frac{(log(x) - \mu_1)^2}{2\sigma_1^2}) \\
&\quad + \frac{1}{\sqrt{2\pi}\sigma_2 x} exp(-\frac{(log(x) - \mu_2)^2}{2\sigma_2^2}).
\end{aligned}$$

Let $\frac{\partial \mathcal{L}(x)}{\partial x} = 0$, then we get x_1 and x_2 as given in Eq. (11.9) are candidates loss points. We observe that Eq. (11.9) can have at most 2 solutions. Furthermore, it can be shown that two different x_1 and x_2 fulfill,

$$x_1 = e^{\frac{-\sqrt{\beta^2 - 4\alpha\gamma} - \beta}{2\alpha}}, \qquad\qquad x_2 = e^{\frac{\sqrt{\beta^2 - 4\alpha\gamma} - \beta}{2\alpha}},$$

where $\beta^2 - 4\alpha\gamma \geq 0$. The optimal threshold is computed as the intersection at $x = x^*$ that fulfills Eq. (11.6), which concludes the proof of Proposition 1.

The variations for the proposed dynamic threshold depend on the recently observed log patterns. In this chapter, during experiments, we record the most recent 10,000 normal event losses and 200 abnormal event losses. We update the threshold whenever more than 20% of the recorded losses change. As such, the loss for model m_1 ranges from 0.1 - 3.1 and the threshold ranges from 0.41 - 0.46. Since normal log data occupied the majority in the whole dataset, more than 80% of the log event losses are clustered between 0.1 - 0.4. Correspondingly, the loss for model m_2 ranges from 0.1 - 3.0 and the threshold ranges from 0.34 - 0.35. Whereas the loss for model m_3 ranges from 0.1 - 2.0 and the threshold ranges from 0.23 - 0.24. In ADA, as the time increases, threshold for each model is updated to adapt to newly observed log patterns.

In Figure 11.4(b) we provide a detailed illustration of the thresholds updated for three different models over a span of 50 time steps where each time step is a composition of 200 log events. Since we employ the proposed adaptive strategy from algorithm 4 during the decision making, the pareto-optimal policy selects the less computationally intensive shallower model m_1 to predict more than 80% of the whole test data. Essentially, we use shallow models for predicting normal data and switch to deeper models only when we detect abnormal data. Therefore m_1's threshold is subjected to more changes than other models. Subsequently, since the observed abnormal events are small, the deeper model m_3 is rarely used and hence, its threshold remained almost stable during testing.

11.3 Chapter summary

In this chapter, we studied the importance of system logs and anomaly detection systems. Essentially, we studied the limitations of existing anomaly detection approaches such as increased computational overhead, latency, failure to detect new threats, etc. We then presented ADA, an adaptive deep log anomaly detection framework for efficiently detecting anomalies in system logs. To overcome the limitations of existing works, we proposed to build online unsupervised models with adaptive model selection and dynamic thresholds for improving latency, reduce computational overhead and dynamic updates. Using pareto-optimal policy we always selected the optimal DNN model with best configurations f or a nomaly d etection a nd thereby, optimally utilized the resources whilst improving the prediction accuracy.

Chapter 12

Application - Cyber Security Data Analysis

In Chapter 9, we proposed *ADA* for efficiently detecting anomalies with online unsupervised deep learning and adaptive model selection strategies. It is paramount for any organization that operates online or uses online services to detect malicious activities such as unauthorized access, malwares, port scanning, *etc*. Many of the attacks allow unauthorized access to the network and could inflict further damages like compromising credentials, violating intellectual property rights, etc. Further, such attacks may even expose business sensitive information including confidential documents of government agencies and could result in serious security breaches [33]. Therefore, system logs are generally used to periodically record states of the systems and any significant events at various significant points to ensure security and detect any potential threats. Nowadays, many computer systems and applications collect and maintain system-wide log data. Analyzing these system logs is essential to discover any potential security breaches and anomalies. Therefore, in this chapter, we analyze the system logs for detecting anomalies as an application to evaluate the performance of the proposed ADA framework. We leverage the Los Alamos National Laboratory (LANL) Cyber Security Dataset [65] to represent the system-log data for evaluating the ADA framework. In particular, we measure the performance of the proposed adaptive model and dynamic threshold and further compare it with the respective state-of-the-art approaches. Evaluations show that ADA accurately detects anomalies with high F1-score (~95%) and it is 97 times faster than existing approaches and incurs very low storage cost.

Contents

12.1 Evaluation

12.1.1 Dataset

The LANL dataset [65] consists of Windows-based system authentication event logs
from LANL's internal computer network. These logs were collected over a period
of 58 consecutive days. The dataset contains over one Billion log entries comprising
of authentication, network flow, DNS lookup events and processes. Privacy related
fields such as users, computers, and processes are anonymized in the dataset.

The network activities recorded in the system logs include both normal operational
network activities as well as a series of abnormal activities termed as the *red team*
activities. The red team activities mainly represent compromised account credentials
over a period of 30 days. In this evaluation, we used the authentication events from
the dataset, and the corresponding statistics are summarized in the Table 12.1.

Table 12.1: **LANL dataset statistics.**

Datasets	Events	Source Computer	Destination Computer
Authentication	1,051,430,459	16,230	15,895
Red team	749	4	301

12.1.2 Experimental setup

In ADA, using the online deep learning similar to the algorithm described by Sahoo
et al. [64], we build multiple ADA-EM DNN models using LSTM and generate

features with LMP [156].

For evaluation, we build four models in ADA with 128, 256, 512 and 1024 LSTM layers and compare them to the state-of-the-art approaches. In order to demonstrate the performance of the models, we limit the scope of the LANL dataset to events recorded on day 8, as it contains the largest number of abnormal events (261) in over seven million system log events. All experiments are performed on a MacBook Pro laptop, with Intel Core i5 CPU at 2.9 GHz and 8 GB (LPDDR3 2133 MHz) of RAM.

12.1.3 Baselines

In this chapter, the proposed ADA framework with the strategies for adaptive model selection and dynamic threshold are employed to build an online unsupervised anomaly detection system. Further, the model m_3 performs optimally in terms of F1-score and latency and hence we select m_3 as the benchmark model in ADA when applying the adaptive algorithm. We compare the performance of this ADA system to the following baselines.

State-of-the-art unsupervised deep learning approaches:

1) NO-ADA: The NO-ADA system is a variant of the ADA framework with online training and unsupervised learning, however, without the adaptive algorithm and dynamic thresholds. The performance of this baseline is obtained with the benchmark model m_3.

2) Fixed-ADA: The Fixed-ADA system is also a variant of the ADA framework with online training and unsupervised learning. In addition, it uses the adaptive strategy shown in algorithm 4 but the threshold of each model is kept constant like NO-ADA.

3) RNNA [119]: The RNNA system uses the state-of-the-art online and unsupervised learning approach where an anomaly detection system is constructed using the LSTM networks with attention algorithm.

4) Kitsune [120]: The Kitsune system uses the state-of-the-art online and unsupervised learning approach that uses the Autoencoder algorithm [160] to differentiate between normal and abnormal events.

5) DAGMM [161]: The DAGMM system uses the state-of-the-art offline unsupervised learning approach called the deep autoencoding gaussian mixture model.

State-of-the-art unsupervised classical learning methods:

1) Isolation Forest (IF) [162]: It is an ensemble-based method for detecting outliers in the dataset.

2) One-class SVM (OCSVM) [163]: It is a max-margin based [164] incremental unsupervised outlier detection model.

3) Self Organizing Maps (SOM) [165]: The SOM networks aim at dividing p-dimensional input space into a finite number of partitions. The whole process is unsupervised and carried out by presenting vectors to all encompassing neurons.

4) Angle-Based Outlier Detection (ABOD) [166]: ABOD detects anomalies by the variance of angles between pairs of data samples.

12.1.4 Metrics

The following metrics are used to evaluate the performance of ADA and the baseline state-of-the-art approaches.

1) F-measure (F1-score): It is the harmonic mean of precision and recall [167] and is given as follows:

$$\text{F1-score} = \frac{2}{\frac{1}{\text{Precision}} + \frac{1}{\text{Recall}}},$$

2) Precision: It is a measure of how many positive instances were identified and it is given as follows:

$$\text{Precision} = \frac{TP}{TP + FP},$$

where TP is True Positives and FP is False Positives.

3) Recall: It is a measure of how many instances were identified correctly and it is given as follows:

$$\text{Recall} = \frac{TP}{TP + FN},$$

where FN is False Negatives.

4) Accuracy: It is a measure of how correctly an anomaly detection system operates by measuring the percentage of TP and True Negatives (TN) along with the number of false alarms in terms of FP and FN that the system produces [168] and is given as follows:

$$\text{Accuracy} = \frac{TP + TN}{TP + FN + FP + TN}.$$

5) Latency: The latency is measured from when a log event is sent as input to the model and until the output prediction is obtained.

12.1.5 Online model performance

To evaluate the performance of ADA, we built four ADA-EM models for the following experiments using online deep learning algorithm similar to sahoo et al. [64]. We begin by training the first model m_1 with 128 LSTM layers followed by the model m_2 with 256 LSTM layers, model m_3 with 512 LSTM layers and the model m_4 with 1024 LSTM layers.

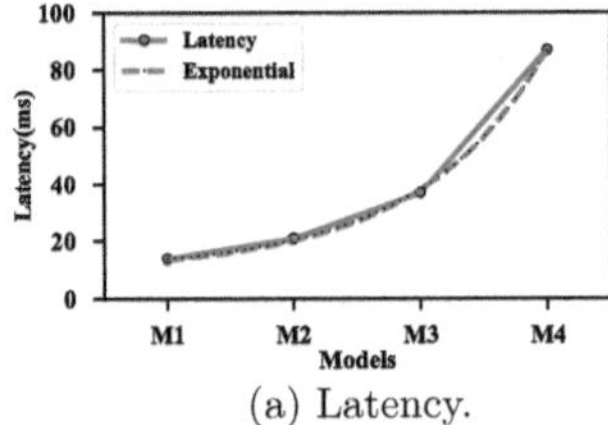

(a) Latency.

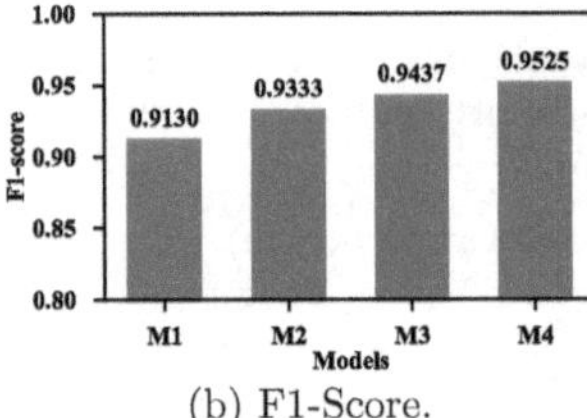

(b) F1-Score.

Figure 12.1: **ADA online model performance.**

To ensure that models built using online deep learning operated efficiently before applying the adaptive strategy from algorithm 4 and dynamic threshold discussed in §11.2 we measured the latency and F1-score of the models. For determine the latency, we measured the execution time incurred by the models for predicting an event and the results are shown in Figure 12.1(a). Noticeably, model m_1 had the lowest latency of 14ms as it had only 128 LSTM layers while model m_4 with 1024 LSTM layers had the highest latency of 87 ms. We noticed that as the number of layers increased, latency increased exponentially.

Further, we also measured the F1-score of the models and results are shown in Figure 12.1(b). We observed that, as the number of layers increased, the depth of

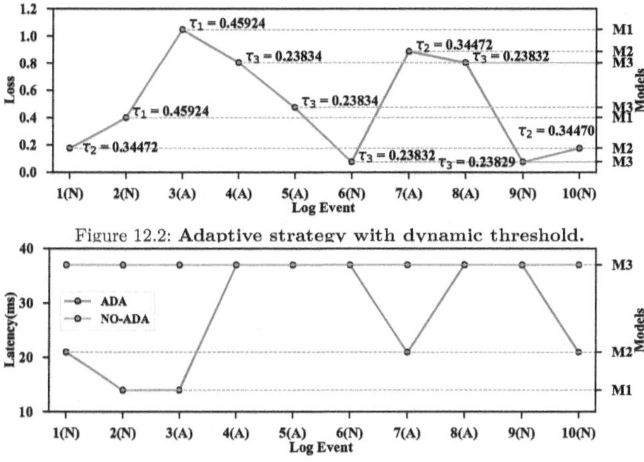

Figure 12.2: **Adaptive strategy with dynamic threshold.**

Figure 12.3: Latency with **ADA** *vs.* **NO-ADA.**

the model also increased and hence the deeper models produced a better F1 score than their shallower counterparts. However, the deeper models have higher latency and demand more computational resources than shallower models. Therefore we only consider models m_1 - m_3 for the evaluation as they had lower latency and produced acceptable F1-scores. Before proceeding further, the proposed adaptive strategy shown in algorithm 4 needed a benchmark model to begin with. Therefore, we selected the model m_2 as our benchmark model by considering the trade-off between accuracy and latency of the three models.

12.1.6 ADA performance

We evaluated the performance of ADA by applying the adaptive strategy from algorithm 4 and dynamic threshold from §11.2 to the models built in the above section. For these experiments, we randomly selected 10 log events and simulated an attack scenario where the events 1-2 show normal authentications and events 3-5 show unauthorized authentications followed by event 6 which is a normal authentication attempt and events 7-8 again perform unauthorized login attempts and finally the events 9-10 display normal authentications. Following the adaptive principle and dynamic threshold, the resulting model used for predicting every event and the corresponding threshold used for distinguishing normal and abnormal events are shown in Figure 12.2 and the normal and abnormal events are indicated on the x-axis with the letters N and A next to events 1-10.

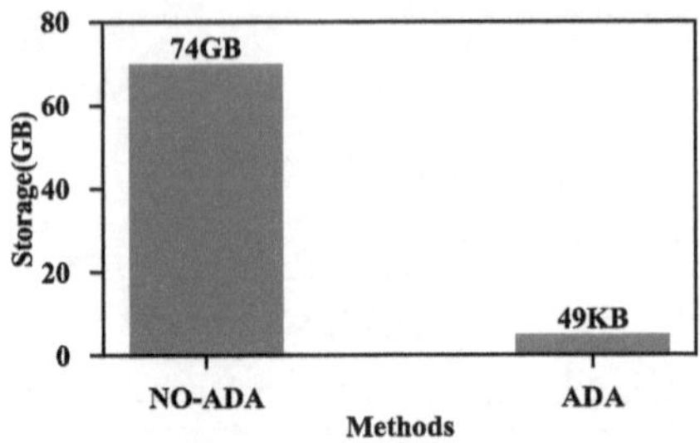

Figure 12.4: **Storage with ADA *vs.* NO-ADA.**

As shown in Figure 12.2, during the initial stage, the benchmark model m_2 was selected for predicting the first event. If this log event was normal, then according to the algorithm 4, the next pareto-optimal model m_1 was selected for predicting the second log event. However, the computationally intensive model m_3 was selected to predict the fourth event to produce high accuracy as the third event was found to be abnormal. The threshold of the model used for prediction is updated and recalculated according to §11.2. Since the number of log events was very small in this experiment, the threshold values did not change that frequently. The results clearly show the benefit of applying the adaptive strategy as the pareto-optimal policy selected shallower models every time a normal event was observed without compromising the identification of abnormal event which were effectively predicted with deeper models to produce higher accuracy.

We also compared the performance of ADA with NO-ADA variant and the results are shown in Figure 12.3. We observed from the results that in NO-ADA, there was no adaptive strategy and hence the pareto-optimal policy selected the deepest DNN model m_3 as it produces the highest accuracy at the cost of increased computational resources and latency. Therefore, with NO-ADA, we achieved an accuracy of 94% at the expense of increased computational resources and latency of 37 ms per log event. However, ADA achieved the accuracy of 91% which is close to m_3 but with less computational resources and 57.6% lower latency.

12.1.7 Storage

Further, we also analyzed that in system logs, the percentage of abnormal events are very low in comparison to normal events. However, due to the necessity to train the anomaly detection models, organizations usually store the data for prolonged periods. Therefore, in Chapter 11, we proposed to store only abnormal data and

Table 12.2: **Fixed threshold *vs.* adaptive threshold.**

Model	F1-score (%)	Accuracy (%)	Recall (%)	Latency (ms)
NO-ADA	94	**94**	**93**	37
Fixed-ADA	91	83	92	18.8
ADA	**95**	91	92	**15.7**

the most recently observed loss values for the normal data and abnormal data. This is sufficient for ADA to accurately predict the behaviours in the system logs and dynamically compute thresholds based on current behaviours. The resulting storage required with ADA in comparison to existing methods which for simplicity we refer to as NO-ADA is shown in Figure 12.4. It is evident that with ADA we incur far less storage cost as we consume just 48 KB of storage for the LANL dataset in comparison to storing the entire 74 GB of the dataset.

For the above mentioned experiments, in Table 12.2 we list the F1-score, accuracy, recall and latency of NO-ADA, Fixed-ADA and ADA variants. We observed that NO-ADA has a good performance in terms of F1-score, accuracy and recall, but at the cost of increased latency due to increased model complexity. Noticeably, ADA achieved the highest F1-score of 95% with the lowest computational latency of 15.7ms among the three variants. Further, the performance of ADA is very close to NO-ADA in terms of accuracy and recall and much better in terms of latency. This is because normal log events occupied a higher percentage in the system log events.

In ADA, due to adaptive strategy shown in algorithm 4, during normal log events the pareto-optimal policy tends to select the model with less computational cost and latency but still produces acceptable accuracy. In ADA, the best model which produces highest accuracy is only employed when abnormal log event appears; as these models demand increased computational resources. The adaptive strategy with fixed threshold also decreases the latency in Fixed-ADA variant. In addition, since the threshold in ADA is updated continuously to adapt to newly observed log patterns in online systems, ADA can achieve higher F1-score compared to that in NO-ADA and Fixed-ADA. Moreover, in Fixed-ADA, we observed that the number of False Positives increased during testing and therefore we used the deeper models more often than in ADA.

12.1.8 Performance comparison

Studies by Mirsky et al. [120] show that offline machine learning algorithms perform considerably better than online machine learning algorithms. Since they have access to the entire dataset during the training, offline algorithms perform multiple passes over the data to build a good model that has learned well. However, constructing neural network models using online algorithm is useful when resources, like the training data, computation and/or memory are limited. Since we utilize online algorithms [64] and enhance the anomaly detection with adaptive model selection and dynamic thresholds, we compared the performance of ADA to both state-of-the-art online and offline algorithms.

In Table 12.3 we summarize the experimental results for the state-of-the-art classical unsupervised machine learning algorithms along with ADA for anomaly detection in system logs. As these classical algorithms use offline learning to train and build the models we used 80% of normal events from day 8 in LANL dataset [65] to train and build models for these algorithms. For testing we used 10,000 normal events from the remaining 20% logs and 200 abnormal events.

Overall, we observed that classical unsupervised machine learning methods demanded very low computational resources and produced results with very less latency of ~0.8 ms. However, due to unbalanced and complex nature of the logged events, their F1-scores are very low in comparison to ADA even though they were pre-trained with the ground-truth.

Table 12.3: **Comparison of machine learning models.**

Model	F1-score (%)	Accuracy (%)	Recall (%)	Latency (ms)
SOM [165]	48	92	33	**0.03**
IF [162]	47	88.3	84.5	0.17
OCSVM [163]	37	60	**95**	0.35
ABOD [166]	25	**95**	27	0.8
ADA	**95**	91	92	15.7

Table 12.4: **Comparison of deep learning models.**

Model	F1-score (%)	Accuracy (%)	Recall (%)	Latency (ms)
RNNA [119]	86	76	78	530
Kitsune [120]	39	64	55	8.6
DAGMM [161]	44	70	47	**0.5**
ADA	**95**	**91**	**92**	15.7

Since ADA is based on unsupervised deep learning, we also compared the performance of ADA with other state-of-the-art deep learning algorithms and the results are given in Table 12.4. Overall, the results presented in Table 12.4 clearly show that ADA outperforms RNNA, Kitsune and DAGMM in terms of F1-score, accuracy and recall. Specifically, t he F 1-score a chieved b y A DA i s a bout 1 1% h igher compared to RNNA and 144% higher compared to Kitsune and 116% higher compared to DAGMM, respectively. With regards to accuracy, RNNA, Kitsune and DAGMM's accuracies are lower than ADA by nearly 16%, 30% and 23%. Whereas, the recall of RNNA, Kitsune and DAGMM are nearly 15%, 40% and 49% less than ADA. As for the latency, RNNA performed the worst since it needed 530ms to predict just one event. This is due to the design of RNNA where they employ user perspective and use a separate LSTM for each user in the dataset. As the number of users increase the overall latency of the system also increases. Although Kitsune and DAGMM had lower latency compared to ADA and RNNA, they did not perform well w.r.t. other metrics. Overall, the evaluations show that ADA efficiently utilizes the available resources, produces highly accurate DNN models and consumes far less resources compared to the state-of-the-art approaches.

12.2 Chapter summary

In this chapter, we evaluated the performance of the ADA framework proposed in Chapter 11. With experiments using the LANL dataset, we demonstrated that ADA significantly improves the performance of anomaly detection in the system logs. In particular, the ADA framework improves the F1-score and latency of anomaly detection in comparison with the state-of-the-art approaches. The experiments also show that ADA decreased the overall storage requirements by efficiently filtering only the abnormal logs for storage.

Chapter 13

Conclusion & Future Prospects

This book presented an analysis of the various heterogeneous and evolving Internet architectures and identified several vital open issues that need to be ad-dressed. The book studied the identified open issues in detail and reinforced the heterogeneous and evolving Internet architectures with efficient solutions. The key contributions of PHOENIX addressed the issues at the application and network levels and has improved the performance, scalability, reliability and optimization challenges accompanying the Internet architectures and their respective application and services.

Contents

13.1 book summary

In PHOENIX, we first analyzed the two most popular naming schemas in ICN: hierarchical *vs.* flat and compared them across interdependent metrics like lookup efficiency, aggregate-ability, semantics and manageability. Our results show that complexity of lookup is higher in hierarchical names, and aggregate-ability looses its benefits with mobility; while mesh-like name spaces can lead to names space explosion. Therefore, we suggested to combine the best-of-both-worlds through leveraging hierarchical semantics at the application layer as it offers benefits of the expressibility and flexibility without the downside of complex name lookups in the network layer. While leveraging flat names at the network layer as they are more suitable for lookups in the FIB to obtain better forwarding efficiency.

We then identified the key requirements of IoT environments and the suitability of ICN architectures to fulfill such requirements in comparison to IP. We also discussed the need for seamless integration of *Sensor Networks* to the Internet to realize IoT and proposed the *ISI* architecture with Gateways to offers the necessary functionality. We further explored Fog computing as an application to implement the *ISI* architecture with a *FOGG* gateway and showed the benefit of proposed architecture with several IoT use cases. We then analyzed the communication patterns in IoT environments and showed that pub/sub is the more common/dominant mode of communication in IoT environments. We discussed the shortcomings of existing ICN solutions like CCN-lite and COPSS to offer the pub/sub capability to IoT and provided a lightweight, inter-operable version of pub/sub named *COPSS-lite* for IoT environments. Through evaluation in a real IoT testbed we showed that IoT environments can significantly benefit with *COPSS-lite*.

We followed this with identifying the need for supporting network mobility in ICN and proposed NeMoI to provide an efficient, robust and reliable mobility architecture to handle network-on-the-move. With distributed *MAs* and logical multi-level FIB, we significantly reduced the routing updates and provided further optimizations to by-pass *MAs* through reactive updates on the path of request flow. Through evaluation on a real world topology we showed that NeMoI significantly reduced the signalling traffic, routing updates, path inflation and packet loss.

We further studied the supervised and unsupervised deep learning models and the need for resource-accuracy optimization. Subsequently, we proposed the architecture EVA with 2-stage deep learning and adaptive strategies for supervised deep learning analysis applications to achieve the desired resource-accuracy trade off and improve performance. Through extensive evaluation with real world surveillance videos, we measured the performance benefits of EVA against state-of-art profiling approaches. The results showed that DNN models created with EVA produced higher accuracies and significantly improved the resource consumption whilst using less bandwidth and storage compared to the state-of-the-art solutions.

Finally, we studied the importance of anomaly detection through unsupervised deep learning models and proposed ADA to use the adaptive strategy and online deep learning with unsupervised deep learning. We further enhanced the detection through deriving a dynamic threshold strategy to account for the uncertainty and evolving threat patterns. Through evaluation of real world cyber security dataset we compared the performance of ADA with the state-of-the-art supervised and un-supervised machine learning approaches. The results showed that ADA significantly

improved the prediction accuracy and latency whilst reducing the computational
overhead and storage compared to state-of-the-art solutions.

13.2 Future prospects

In PHOENIX, we have observed the evolution of Internet architectures from IP
towards IPv6, ICN and IoT and we provided efficient solutions to address the many
identified problems. However, the growing number of Internet users introduces many
new challenges like scalability, latency, traffic, limited bandwidth, congestion, cost,
etc. The traffic in the core network is already a concern and hence there is a
growing consensus to utilize Edge/Fog computing to bring the computation closer
to the source and limit the bandwidth in the core network. The emerging new
applications and technologies like AI, Big Data, Data Analytic, HD videos, *etc.*,
generate TeraBytes of data/day and rely on computing services like data analysis
provided in the Cloud. The current design of Internet and the future architectures
like ICN and IoT are not equipped to handle such large volumes of data. The
benefits like caching offered by ICN, will soon be rendered ineffective by transmitting
such large amount of data in the network, IoT devices cannot store/transmit such
continuous and large volumes of data, the current design of IP is already facing
congestion with the traffic from video applications (60% of total Internet traffic),
the data traffic from AI applications will aggravate the problems.

Therefore, we need to expedite the research in this field and implement the solutions to match the rate of emerging new applications and the growing needs of users.
However, this is not an easy task, as current technologies and architectures were not
designed for such bandwidth and resource hungry applications. Further, the rapid
increase in the number of users and intelligent devices (mobile, IoT) that use Internet have shed the light on the inability of the existing networking infrastructure to
fulfill the needs of the users and the applications. We need to rethink the design of
networking architectures and protocol to provide efficient solutions and not overlay
solutions as quick fixes. We believe that there is a great room for progress and many
new innovative research challenges like naming schema, global time synchronization
in IoT domain, mobility, security, communication protocol, *etc.*, are still open to
the research community to tackle. In this regard, we will continue to explore this
field of research and extend the work done in Chapter 3 with structural analysis, the
work done in Chapter 4 with performance evaluations and discuss our observations.
Further, we also wish to focus on optimizing the bandwidth utilization during video
transmission in mobile environments like 5G to improve the QoE of the users and
achieve fairness w.r.t. competing flows. We also wish to apply our rate adaptive

strategies to WSN and IoT applications to explore the limitations of these networks
and devices w.r.t DNNs and optimize their performance and resource utilization.

13.3 book impact

The contents in PHOENIX have been published in the following peer-reviewed jour-
nals and conference proceedings:

The analysis on the impact of naming schema on the performance of ICN protocols
in Chapter 3 was published in the following conference proceedings:

(i) **Comparison** [169]- **Adhatarao, S.**, Chen, J., Arumaithurai, M., Fu, X.
and Ramakrishnan, KK. Comparison of naming schema in ICN. In Proceedings of the IEEE international symposium on local and metropolitan
area networks (LANMAN'16), Rome, Italy, Jun 13-15, 2016. Accessible

The proposal for seamless integration of heterogeneous *Sensor Networks* to the
Internet in Chapter 4&5 were published in the following journal and conference
proceedings:

(ii) **ISI** [170]- **Adhatarao, S.**, Arumaithurai, M., Kutscher, D. and Fu, X. ISI:
Integrate sensor networks to Internet with ICN. In Proceedings of the IEEE
Internet of Things Journal (IoT'18), Aug 18, 2017. Accessible at:

(iii) **FOGG** [171]- **Adhatarao, S.**, Arumaithurai, M. and Fu, X. FOGG: A fog
computing based gateway to integrate sensor networks to Internet. In Proceedings of the IEEE International Teletraffic Congress (ITC'17), Genoa, Italy,
Sep 4-8, 2017. Accessible

The proposal for a light-weight publish/subscribe system for IoT in Chapter 6 is
under review in the following conference proceedings:

(iv) **COPSS-lite** [172]- **Adhatarao, S.**, Wang, H., Arumaithurai, M. and Fu, X.
COPSS-lite: A Lightweight ICN based Pub/Sub System for IoT Environments.
In Proceedings of the IEEE International Conference on Mobility, Sensing and
Networking (MSN'20), Tokyo, Japan, Dec 17-19, 2020.

The proposal to provide network mobility in ICN in Chapter 7&8 were published
in the following journal and conference proceedings:

(v) **NeMoI: Extended** [173]- **Adhatarao, S.**, Arumaithurai, M., Kutscher, D.
and Fu, X. NeMoI: Network mobility in ICN. In Proceedings of the Springer
Lecture Notes in Computer Science (LNCS'18), December 31, 2018. Accessible
at: `https://link.springer.com/bookseries/558`

(vi) **NeMoI** [174]- **Adhatarao, S.**, Arumaithurai, M., Kutscher, D. and Fu, X.
NeMoI: Network mobility in ICN. In Proceedings of the IEEE International
Conference on Communication Systems & Networks (COMSNETS'18), Ben-
galuru, India, Jan 3-7, 2018. Accessible at: `https://link.springer.com/`
`chapter/10.1007/978-3-030-10659-1_10`

The proposal to provide resource-accuracy optimization with supervised deep learning models in Chapter 9&10 is under submission (under re-submission after 1st
round of reviews) in the following journal:

(vii) **EVA** [175]- **Adhatarao, S.**, Prasad, A., Arumaithurai, M. and Fu, X. EVA:
A Distributed Optimization Architecture for Efficient Video Analysis. In Proceedings of the IEEE Transactions on Mobile Computing (TMC'20). *Under
2nd round revision.*

The proposal to provide real-time security with unsupervised deep learning models
in Chapter 11&12 was published in the following journal and conference proceedings:

(viii) **ADA** [176]- Yuan, Y. *, **Adhatarao, S.** *, Lin, M., Yuan, Y., Liu, Z. and
Fu, X. ADA: Adaptive Deep Log Anomaly Detector. In Proceedings of the
IEEE Conference on Computer Communications (INFOCOM'20), Toronto,
Canada, July 6-9, 2020. * **Joint First Author**. Accessible at: `https:`
`//ieeexplore.ieee.org/abstract/document/9155487`